The Bradford Pals

I dedicate this book to the late George Morgan of Bradford, Yorkshire, formerly a Sergeant in 'B' Company, the 16th Battalion of the West Yorkshire Regiment, without whose assistance it would never have been written. As were his comrades, a brave and patriotic man, the like of whom we may never see again.

The Bradford Pals

A short history of the 16th and 18th (Service) Battalions of the Prince of Wales Own West Yorkshire Regiment; based on the War Diaries of the Battalions and the experiences of the men who served in them from August, 1914, to February, 1918.

by

Ralph N. Hudson

2nd edition

Bradford Libraries
Arts Museums and Libraries Division
City of Bradford Metropolitan Council

ISBN 0 907734 38 3

1st edition published by the author in 1977.

2nd edition published by Bradford Libraries,
Central Library,
Princes Way,
Bradford.
BD1 1NN.

Printed by Alden Press in 12 point Times Roman.

TABLE OF CONTENTS

LIST OF ILLUSTRATIONS

LIST OF MAPS

Notes on Map References:

At the time of the First World War, British Army maps were divided into large squares bearing large letters, A, B. C, D, etc. These squares were sub-divided into small squares numbered 1 to 30 or 1 to 36, depending on the scale. These squares were further sub-divided into four minor squares identified, left to right a, b, c, d, the sides of which were then divided by ten.

Thus, to find the location of map reference C30b 6.9, one found the large square 'C', then the small square 30, then the sub-division 'b'. Finally, counting six-tenths west to east and eight-tenths south to north, one arrived at the exact location on the map.

ACKNOWLEDGEMENT:

The author wishes to express his grateful thanks to Mr. George Sassoon for allowing him to use verses written by his father, Siegfried Sassoon. Quotations are from "The War Poems", published by Faber and Faber Ltd., 1983.

The author acknowledges his debt to the Imperial War Museum for allowing photographs from their collection to be reproduced, to the Ministry of Defence and the Prince of Wales's Own Regiment of Yorkshire for permission to reproduce their Crown Copyright MOD listings of officers and men killed in the War, and to the Telegraph and Argus for permission to reproduce their photographs.

I would also like to thank the following Bradford Libraries' staff: Dot Jackson for scanning the original, Bob Duckett and Elvira Willmott for the Reading List, Kate Mellalieu for the cover design and Robert Walters for putting it all together.

AUTHOR'S PREFACE:

I grew up in the shadow of two battalions. In an age when many young women did not marry because there were not enough men to go around. People spoke of the Somme, and of the 'Pals', almost in a whisper.

I grew up in a town, like many other northern towns in that time, which had lost its best young men.

When I was younger, I was too busy with my own affairs to worry myself too much with the dying of these young men, probably even more interested in another war of my own time. As I approached an age when I would be too old to fight, but my son approached an age when he would, I became appalled by the implications of war and particularly the destruction of these two battalions. I resolved to find out what had really happened to them.

This short book is an attempt to record their story.

NOTE FROM THE PUBLISHERS:

Mr Hudson's book has been out of print for some years. It was written with the benefit of the author's close friendship with many of the survivors, and with the full co-operation of the Bradford Pals Old Comrades' Association. It provides an important link with the Pals themselves, and acts as a testament to their courage, generosity and spirit. It is written in a language and an idiom which they would have recognised, much of it being in their own words.

Therefore when the author offered to allow Bradford Libraries to publish a 2nd edition we realised the importance of being able to make it available once more.

The 2nd edition contains substantial textual additions by the author, many amendments made on the basis of surviving Pals' comments upon the original edition, as well as additional background documentation and an index of names and places.

FOREWORD BY LESLIE SANDS

In that grim autumn of 1914, the young men came from everywhere to take the King's shilling and to offer him their dedicated services. From mills and mines, from office chairs and civic departments, from loom and bench and lathe and counter, they flooded the recruiting centres in answer to the nation's call for young manhood. With a patriotic fervour rarely equalled in the annals of our history, these lads

No 16/568 Sgt. Albert Edward Sands, 16th Bn., served 1914-1919, father of Leslie Sands.

turned themselves from a citizens' army into a highly skilled professional fighting force whose determination and fortitude would earn them the admiration of the world. The Pals' Battalions, in Bradford and elsewhere, gave all their physical and mental energies in a total commitment to the preservation of the homeland and the defence of assaulted freedom. In the case of the Bradford Pals, the majority also gave their lives.

Those few who came back (for the two battalions of volunteers were "thrice decimated in battle") rarely talked to outsiders about their part in what came to be known as "The Great War". They had seen what was left of their youth and their ideals destroyed in the mud and filth of Flanders; and disillusion and moral betrayal are not favoured topics of conversation among war veterans because they represent a waste of precious time.

One thing stayed intact for these survivors, one single factor that had sustained them all through the horrors of the Western Front and remained with them now, to give some consolation in the post-war days of bitter recrimination and reassessment. The Pals were a close circle that denied all intrusion, but there was a bond between each and every one of them that would never be severed. They treasured - and guarded jealously - the golden bond of comradeship. They had been aptly named.

Bradford has always honoured the First and Second Pals Battalions. It owes a debt of gratitude now to the author of this book, Mr. Ralph Hudson, who has worked tirelessly with application, understanding and compassion, to ensure that their glory and their tragedy are kept vividly alive for us nearly eighty years later. We who came after must revere them, for we inherited the privilege of their memory and the freedom that meant the sacrifice of an entire generation - the day before yesterday.

Leslie Sands, 1993.

George Morgan

Physical training, Manningham Park, 1914.

CHAPTER 1: IN THE BEGINNING

*Soldiers are men of action; they must win
Some flaming, fatal climax with their lives.*
Siegfried Sassoon

Much has been written about the flood of volunteers who, in a mood of crusading idealism, answered Field-Marshal Kitchener's call to arms in 1914. So overwhelming was their response that the Regular Army, until then of small establishment, approximately 125,000 men, was completely unable to absorb the numbers involved. To resolve this problem and to satisfy the zeal of the would-be volunteers, who felt unable to accept long delays before they joined the colours, many towns formed 'Citizens' Army Leagues'. These leagues, on obtaining the approval of the War Office, raised their own battalions and bore the cost of clothing, feeding and training them until such time as the War Office could absorb them into regular formations. A leading Bradfordian, Sir W. E. B. Priestly, M.P., led a group of prominent Bradford business men to seek permission of Field-Marshal Kitchener to form such a league. Permission being granted, the *Bradford Citizens' Army League* was formed on the 20th September, 1914, with its depot at 23 Bridge Street and the Lord Mayor as Chairman.

1

Volunteers rushed to enlist. Men of all ages from mid-teens to mid-forties besieged the recruiting office, established at the Mechanics Institute, where the band of the 2nd 6th (Reserve) Battalion of the West Yorkshire Regiment played patriotic tunes and marching music, and where a Sergeant Major besported himself in full 'Regimentals'.

The Bradford Telegraph told its readers "The special inducement of the new Bradford Service battalion is that young men shall be enrolled to serve, shoulder to shoulder, with their friends and colleagues in civil life".

Standards in physique and intelligence were set very high. Men were rejected for the slightest physical defect. Mr. George Morgan, one of the first to volunteer, was asked his age by a Recruiting Sergeant. When he replied that he was sixteen the Sergeant advised him "You had better go outside, come back again and tell me something different". He recalled "I came back in and told him that I was nineteen and I was in. When I told my mother that I had joined up, she said that I was a fool and she'd give me a good hiding, but I said 'I'm a man now and you can't hit a man'". Mr. Arthur Wadsworth was so disgusted at being rejected because of his age - he was also sixteen - that he walked to Leeds and joined the 'Leeds Pals', this time suitably revising his age. Within a week 1,000 volunteers had been accepted into the battalion.

However, a battalion cannot be formed from raw recruits alone, it needs officers and N.C.O.s. These positions were, in the main, filled by retired officers and reservists known as 'Dug-outs', together with what the War Office chose to describe as 'suitably qualified young men'. The latter were usually young volunteers whose sole experience of the martial arts had been one afternoon per week with the 'Officer Cadet Corps' of the local grammar school, shy young men in new, well-cut clothes, spiral puttees, stiff new Sam

Brown belts and brown boots: officers' breeches at £2.12s.6d., tunic at £3.7s.6d. from Pope & Bradley......

Some of the 'Dug-outs' appear to have had difficulty in ridding these young Bradfordians of what was seen as a rather casual

Captain Blagbrough and Lieutenant Robinson instructing recruits, Manningham Park, 1914

attitude towards military etiquette. A soldier rebuked for not saluting an officer is said to have replied "but I know him!"

Other 'Dug-outs' had trouble with local dialect. An officer who asked a soldier why he was not wearing his cap on parade was rather perplexed by the reply: "Arz bart".

The battalion was to be known, officially, as the 16th battalion, the Prince of Wales Own West Yorkshire Regiment. Locally it was known as 'The Bradford Pals' and later, when the Citizens' Army League were able to cope with the organization of a second battalion, as the 'First Bradford Pals'.

For the first three months the battalion made its Headquarters at the skating rink which, until recent years, stood on Manningham Lane, drilled in the local parks with obsolescent Long Lee-Enfield rifles, but returned home each evening to sleep. For this they were paid a food and lodging allowance of 21 shillings per week (£1.05 in decimal currency). A private soldier's pay was 7 shillings per week (approximately 35 pence). From this he would be expected to make an allotment of 3 shillings and 6 pence (about 17 pence) to his next of kin. This would be made up in the case of an allotment to a mother to 10 shillings and tu' pence (approximately 51 pence) by the Army. Thus, the

3

spending power of the private soldier was 3 shillings and 6 pence per week (17 pence), from which he would be expected to supply such needs as soap, shaving materials, toothpaste, boot polish and metal polish (for cleaning buttons and cap badges, etc.). Each man was issued with two blue uniforms of the best worsted which Bradford's looms could weave, one of which had silver buttons bearing the city's coat of arms. As with other Citizens' Army Leagues throughout the country, the citizens of Bradford bore the total costs and expenses of the battalion.

On January 14th, 1915, the 'First Pals' marched to Skipton where they were to be accommodated in a purpose-built camp. The *Bradford Daily Telegraph* commented on the prevailing weather, "A more unpropitious day for the Bradord Pals to march to their new quarters in Skipton could not have happened", being a day of high winds and heavy showers. Their march began from the Town Hall Square where they were inspected by the Lord Mayor. The 'ARGUS', describing the scene, said they had "displayed themselves as a body of fit, smart, purposeful manhood". When all farewells were said, the order rang out from their commanding officer, Colonel G. H. Muller, seated on his white charger, and they marched off in style. Their route took them via Blubberhouses Moor, where they spent the night in improvised accommodation. 'B' Company bedded down in the local church hall where George Morgan, now a member of this company had to sleep on the top of the piano, such was the shortage of space.

The 'League' now felt sufficiently confident to contemplate a second battalion, and in February, 1915, the 'Second Bradford Pals' was formed. This battalion was officially designated the 18th (Service) Battalion, the Prince of Wales Own West Yorkshire Regiment. The 'Second Pals' established themselves under canvas in Bowling Park. Alfred Scott had joined the First Pals in September, 1914, and was training with them at Skipton.

However, Alfred Scott had a elder brother, a former regular in the Coldstream Guards and a reservist who had been called to the colours. When he was posted to the Second Pals as Regimental Sergeant Major he 'claimed' his younger brother, and had him transferred to his own battalion, presumably to be

Rifle drill in Manningham Park, 1914. Albert Sands, front row on the left.

able to "keep an eye own him!!" Thus Alfred Scott had the distinction of serving both battalions. The career of Sergeant Major H. Scott is described in some detail in Richard Alford's book *On the word of command....*

The reserves of the two battalions were brought together at the Bowling Park camp towards the end of May and, by process of evolution they progressed towards independent status. In July they moved to Colsterdale to join the reserves of the two battalions which had been raised in Leeds, to form the 19th (Local Reserve) Battalion West Yorkshire Regiment. However the reserves of these four battalions became too bulky to handle as one unit so the reserves of the 16th and 18th battalions were moved to Clipstone in Nottinghamshire where they became the 20th Battalion West Yorkshire Regiment. These reserve companies were, initially, made up of men from serving battalions who were seen as unfit for foreign service. Later some of these men were discharged whilst others were transferred to the 1st Yorkshire Garrison Regiment for home service. The remainder formed the actual reserves who would be drafted as replacements for casualties in the service battalions.

The Citizens' Army League was, in fact, pressured by the War Office in January 1915 to raise another battalion of men qualified to perform a dual role of Pioneers and Infantry. Initially the League took the view that the Bradford area was not suitable for this purpose. When the request was repeated in August the League agreed to combine with other West Riding authorities to raise such a battalion. This was to be known as the 21st Service (Pioneer) Battalion West Yorkshire Regiment.

In May, 1915, the 16th and 18th Battalions marched to Ripon, and, swapping their blue uniforms for regulation khaki, were absorbed into the Regular Army.

Initially both battalions formed part of the original 31st Division which included the 12th Battalion the York and Lancaster Regiment (known as the Sheffield City Battalion as featured in J. Harris' book *Covenant with Death*), the 13th and 14th Battalions the York and Lancaster Regiment (the 1st and 2nd Barnsley Pals), the 11th Battalion the East Lancashire Regiment (the Accrington Pals) and the 12th Battalion the King's Own Yorkshire Light Infantry (the Halifax Pals). However, in the early part of the war, Lord Kitchener seems to have looked upon his 'New Army' divisions as a source of replacement brigades and not to have seriously considered training them as fully operational formations.

In April, 1915, the original 31st Division was broken up into independent brigades for draft-finding purposes. Subsequently in September, 1915, both battalions moved, as part of the 93rd Infantry Brigade, to Fovant in Wiltshire where they were issued with tropical kit which included pith helmets, lengths of muslin called 'pugarees' (to be wound around the helmet as an insulator) and grey flannel body belts. They also exchanged their Long Lee-Enfields with short bayonets for the current active service rifle, the Mark 3 short Lee-Enfield with its 18" bayonet, although they still retained their obsolete leather belts with leather ammunition pouches worn on each side. Each pouch could contain a bandolier of fifty rounds and two clips each of five rounds.

The 93rd Infantry Brigade was composed of the 15th (Leeds Pals), the 16th and 18th Battalions of the West Yorkshire Regiment, and the 18th Battalion of the Durham Light Infantry

Young recruits, three still in their blue uniforms, Harry Severn on the left.

(Durham Pals). Before leaving Fovant they were inspected by a ruddy faced General, a 'Dug-out',who advised, with tears in his eyes that they should "Trust in God and keep your rifles clean".

On December 6th they entrained for a destination kept secret at the time from 'other ranks' which proved to be Liverpool Docks. They embarked on the Canadian Pacific steamship *Empress of Britain,* a vessel of some 14,000 tons displacement, designed to carry 1550 passengers in peacetime.The ship had been converted to a trooper by removing most of its passenger cabins which opened up large areas between decks where large numbers of hammocks could be slung from the deckhead. Beneath the hammocks were tables and bench seats where meals were to be taken. When not in use enamel mugs and plates were stored on the tables. Troops were only to be allowed on deck barefoot, as it was considered that Army boots in such numbers would not be conducive to the care of the wooden decks. Additional lavatory accommodation which had been installed in the well decks was to prove woefully inadequate with results that can only be left to the imagination.

They left the Mersey accompanied by two Royal Navy destroyers, but by the next morning these escorts had disappeared. By the afternoon of the fourth day *The Empress* was steaming in wide circles to the west of Gibraltar, waiting for nightfall before passing through the Straits.

Soon after midnight with Gibraltar safely behind them the *Empress* proceeded at her normal speed. All was quiet below decks save for the throb of the engines and the creaking of the hull, when suddenly men were aroused from their sleep by a loud, high-pitched mechanical screech coming from the bowels of the ship. Almost simultaneously there was the sensation of the hull colliding, bows on, with a large obstacle. For a moment the *Empress* rocked violently from side to side, mugs and other loose objects cascading from the tables and clattering on to the decks. Then all was silence, not even the throb of the engines to be heard. The silence between decks was soon broken as men fumbled for clothes and life jackets in the semi-darkness, the only illumination being provided by the low power electric 'night lights' which were mounted on the bulkheads.

After a few moments two officers came down the companion ways to reassure everyone that all was well, saying that the ship had been in collision with a fishing boat. In view of the violence of the impact, many thought this an unlikely story. However, about 30 minutes later the welcome throb of the engines was heard again and the ship proceeded on its way. It was learned the next day that the so-called fishing boat had, in fact, been the French steamer *Djingjurd* with some sixty souls on board, two of whom were killed. All the rest were safely taken on board the *Empress*. The *Djingjurd* sank within twenty minutes of the collision.

The *Empress* proceeded to Malta for a short stay while the damaged bows were inspected, and then resumed her journey east. None of the 'other ranks' had been told of her destination, prompting much speculation whether they were heading for Gallipoli, where fighting still raged, or perhaps India?

On December 18th, off Cyprus, a U-boat was sighted some miles to starboard. Two shots were fired from the ship's gun, causing the U-boat to dive. Almost immediately another U-boat was sighted some two thousand yards to port. This boat followed the example of its companion, without attempting any warlike act. Each of these incidents, had fate decreed, could have proved more catastrophic than the fate which awaited them in the crater fields of France.

On December 21st they sailed into the wide expanse of Alexandria harbour, and anchored for the night. From thence there only remained the short voyage to Port Said where both battalions finally disembarked on December 22nd, 1915. The following day the 16th Battalion despatched 'C' Company, under the command of Captain Blagbrough, to an outpost at Ras-el-Aish. The rest of the Battalion, together with the 18th, remained in Port Said until January 1st, 1916. These first few days in Egypt were spent in a tented camp a short distance outside Port Said, near enough for the men to explore the sights and shops of the town. Bathing parades were especially enjoyed when the battalions were marched to the nearby beaches to plunge into the inviting waters of the Mediterranean, needless to say, without bothering too much about the lack of bathing costumes.

Their next destination was Kantara, a small town on the east

Bradford Pals under training at Ripon. Albert Sands is 4th from left, front row.

bank of the Suez Canal, in those days little more than a railway station and a few other buildings. From here they moved into the desert to a location known as 'Point 70' where they were employed on outpost duties and the construction of defences. The purpose of these was to protect the northern caravan routes from the Turks. The day after their arrival, a 'Drum Head' service was conducted for the 18th Battalion by their chaplain, the Reverend Thornton who, in peacetime, was a curate at Bradford Parish Church (now Bradford Cathedral). He told the men that they were standing on the caravan route from Palestine to Egypt, probably the route which Christ took on his journey into Egypt.

Life here was tedious and uncomfortable. The Pals learned to suffer heat, dirt, flies, scorpions and camel spiders. Water was strictly rationed, being brought in by camel train. Each man received one gallon a day which had to suffice for cooking and washing as well as for drinking.

Food was monotonous, if not poor. Normal army rations of that time were converted to 'desert rations' at the following scale:

Standard army rations	Desert rations
1lb of meat	1lb of preserved meat (bully beef)
1lb of fresh bread	1lb of biscits or 3/4lb of flour
1/50lb of mustard	1/8lb of curry powder
4oz of fresh vegetables	2oz of rice or 3oz of potatoes or 4oz of onions
Cheese	Condensed milk at the rate of 1 tin per 16 men

The biscuits were approximately round in shape, about three inches in diameter and about a half inch thick. They were so hard that it was impossible to eat them unless they were first soaked in tea or stew. The general opinion was that they had been stored as surplus from some long-forgotten colonial war.

One day the Divisional Commander paid them a visit. George Morgan was on a trench digging detail when he arrived. He approached the detail, mounted on his horse, dressed in immaculately laundered and pressed khaki and gleaming riding boots, and asked: 'Have you any complaints?' Lance Corporal Gee spoke up, saying 'We don't get enough to eat, Sir'. The Divisional Commander glared down at the Lance Corporal and said, in a sarcastic tone: "Well, you certainly look very well on it." Life in George Morgan's platoon was made more bearable by the presence of Private George Harrison who seemed able to turn his hand to anything. When sand storms blew down other tents, their's would stand. George would have gone out and driven in the pegs before the storm struck. The platoon motto became 'leave it to George'. Other characters in the platoon were Owen Moor who was always to be found 'doing someone a favour'; Bill Kenny, a Roman Catholic, who had studied for the priesthood - he was regarded as the platoon philosopher; Squire Clough, a quiet young man from a wealthy family - he became engaged to the Mayor of Pudsey's daughter before leaving England; Billy Booth, a close friend of George Morgan, and Dawson Horne, the platoon comedian, who entertained everyone with stories of how he intended to rout the enemy single handed.

Private J. Patchet of 'A' Company was caught after lights out in his tent writing a letter by candlelight. He was ordered to extinguish the light and turn in. Feeling this to be unreasonable, he continued to write. Private Patchet therefore found himself on a charge and up before the Colonel. Now Private Patchet was, in civilian life, a solicitor and, in this instance, considered the charge to be unreasonable and himself innocent. Therefore when asked if he would accept the Colonel's punishment he demanded a Court Martial. The Army granted his request. Later a Field-Court Martial awarded him two years hard labour.

Captain Smith of 'B' Company rebuked one of his men for writing an 'indecent letter' which the Captain had to censor. Surprised at this accusation the soldier asked what part of his letter, written to a workmate, was offensive. Captain Smith sternly pointed to a paragraph in which the soldier had written: "Since I've been in Egypt, I've had some forbidden fruit!!!"

The activity which, after digging trenches, more frequently absorbed the rest of the battalion's time was to prevent local Arabs stealing their kit, a task to which they applied themselves with zeal.

Very lights over the Somme. *Imperial War Museum, Negative Q1208.*

CHAPTER 2: EARLY DAYS IN FRANCE

I cannot hear their voices, but I see
Dim candles in the barn: they gulp their tea,
And soon they'll sleep like logs. Ten miles away
The battle winks and thuds in blundering strife.
And I must lead them nearer, day by day,
To the foul beast of war that bludgeons life.
Siegfried Sassoon.

At the beginning of 1916, Field-Marshal Haig's plans for a grand offensive by the British on the western front were nearing completion. The 93rd Infantry Brigade was ordered to France to join, as part of the new 31st Division, the largest army ever fielded by Great Britain, an army composed entirely of volunteers.

The Brigade sailed from Port Said on February 29th, 1916, aboard the S.S. *Minneapolis*, a vessel fated to be lost to a U-boat attack on its return voyage. They disembarked in Marseilles on March 6th and marched from the docks to railway sidings where they boarded some ramshackle wagons marked 'Quarante Hommes ou Huit Chevaux'. The train began its journey north at a leisurely pace, the weather becoming bitterly cold as time passed. So recently accustomed to sunny climes the men had only iron rations and the contents of their water bottles to sustain them. From time to time they passed French ambulance trains carrying wounded from Verdun to hospitals in the South.

On March 9th, they reached their destination, Pont Remy, a railhead near Abbeville. The following day the 16th Battalion marched to Merelessart, the 18th Battalion to Citerne, where they were to remain for two weeks. The march was not to be recalled with pleasure by anyone. The weather was still bitterly cold and, added to this, it began to snow as the battalions marched off. The marching was hard going over the rough road cobble *pave*. Fifty minutes of marching would be followed by ten minutes rest. Covering nine to twelve miles a day, they slept at night in barns on filthy straw with the smell of open middens. As they got closer to the forward areas, night illuminations held their gaze; in their ears was the sound of heavy detonations.

There followed a period of training and general familiarization. During this period a party of officers and N.C.O.'s of the 16th Battalion were attached to units in the front line to gain first hand experience in the trenches. These were:

Captain F. Holmes	Captain G. S. Blagbrough
Captain A. Clough	Captain R. W. A. Pringle
Captain H. Russell	Lieutenant S. L. F. Hoffman
Lieutenant R. Sutcliffe	Lieutenant C. T. Ransome
2nd Lieut. J.M.H. Hoffman	2nd Lieutenant F. 0. Brumley
2nd Lieutenant P. C. Parker	2nd Lieutenant C. F. Claxton
Company Q. M. S. Hicks	Corporal Moor
Sergeant Watson	Corporal Flood
Sergeant Binclark	Corporal McConnel
Sergeant Ambler	Corporal Newton
Sergeant W. Morgan	Corporal Nelson
Sergeant Sowden	Corporal Owen
Sergeant Buttler	Lance Corporal Woodhouse
Sergeant Saville	Lance Corporal Burgoyne
Sergeant Dodsworth	Lance Corporal Shackleton
Sergeant Pullen	Lance Corporal Corless
Sergeant Manley	

To gain experience in trench work 'half companies' of the 18th Battalion were attached to the 18th Battalion of the Durham Light Infantry who were in the front line at that time.

On March 25th, both battalions began a march towards the Beaumont-Hamel area, resting each night in villages en-route.

They finally went into billets in Bus-les-Artois at the beginning of April. Here the rolling plains of Picardy reminded many of the 'Pals' of their native Yorkshire.

The 18th Battalion lost their Commanding Officer, Lieutenant-Colonel E. C. H. Kennard, when he departed for England on April 18th. His place was taken by Major, acting Lieutenant-Colonel, M. N. Kennard. Captain, acting Major, Carter was second-in-command of the Battalion. The 16th Battalion was, at that time, commanded by Major E. C. Kennedy.

Private Jimmy F. Hogson, killed by sniper in 1916.

At this point it is well worth considering the comments of Mr. George Taylor, then a private soldier in the 18th Battalion and later a recipient of a 'Field Commission', regarding the standard of training. Both battalions had been taught 'magazine rapid fire', each man being able to put fifteen aimed shots in one minute on to a four foot square target at three hundred yards range. At this they had reached a very high standard. Their route-marching was also second to none. Unfortunately route marching was to prove of little use in the coming holocaust whilst 'magazine rapid fire' was only of use in defence. All the junior officers were completely inexperienced. But both battalions did now enjoy the atmosphere of a somewhat exclusive club. An example of the prevailing spirit is to be found in the case of Private Jimmy Hodgson, George Morgan's cousin. Jimmy Hodgson ruptured himself during training but refused an offer of a discharge and demanded an operation so that he could "stay with the battalion." Knowing this, his comrades would insist that the heavier parts of his equipment were "shared amongst the platoon" when route marching, etc. In point of fact, George Morgan helped to carry his equipment into the line of June 30th, the night before the beginning of the Somme offensive. Jimmy Hodgson was killed by a sniper after July 1st. The Bradford-born author, Mr. J. B. Priestley, was later to describe these men, and those of other 'New Army' battalions, as the intellectual and physical elite of the nation.

On April 20th, at 5.00 p.m., the 16th Battalion marched from Bus-les-Artois and relieved the 10th Battalion, the East Yorkshire Regiment, in the trenches near Colin Camps. 'A', 'C' and 'D' Companies, under Captains Pringle and Blagbrough and Major Moor, occupied the front line. 'B' company, under Captain Holmes formed the reserve. The 18th Battalion had, on the previous day, occupied the right sub-sector south of the Serre Road, facing Redan Ridge and the Quadrilateral Redoubt.

Now began their apprenticeship in the art of war. Tours of duty usually consisted of four days in the front line, followed by four days in the support trenches, followed by a spell in reserve.

The front line here was well dug in hard ground and divided into short bays as protection against enfilade fire, with fire steps for manning the parapet. It was well protected by belts of barbed wire along the front a few yards into No-Man's Land, which was about 200 yards wide hereabouts. They were cold and wet, and smelt of poisonous gas, from gas shells, of explosives, and of the latrines.Ever present was the sickly sweet smell of decaying human flesh coming from the corpses which lay unburied in No-Man's Land. During the day front line duty consisted primarily in maintaining a watch by periscope for enemy activity, in carrying out any necessary repairs to the trench, and in weapon cleaning. The main activities on both sides took place at night when wiring parties were sent out with appropriate covering arrangements by more men further out. Patrols were despatched to investigate the enemy barbed wire defences, to gather intelligence and to be alert to the presence of enemy patrols. For those taking part in these activities feelings varied depending on individual strength of nerve when approaching the German wire, but to some extent these were replaced by the sheer exasperation of having to manipulate coils of barbed wire and corkscrew stakes over churned up ground in darkness whilst making futile efforts not to make a noise. Not surprisingly, in total contrast to the apprehension felt marching towards the front line to take over, would be the sensation of the return to security once the trench was regained after the uncertainties of No-Man's Land. Out there was always the possibility of being stalked, like game, by an enemy patrol, or of a machine gun opening up in the vicinity.

Both sides used Very lights at night, apart from when they had patrols or working parties out in front. As a result, with experience, the amount of activity taking place in one's vicinity could be judged by the presence, or otherwise, of Very lights overhead. The Germans also used parachute flares which illuminated the ground underneath, and hung in the air much longer than did the Very lights. Both sides also used coloured rockets to signal emergencies. The sensation of being clearly exposed to view when standing upright in No-man's land was almost overwhelming at first. Complete immobility was found to be the best protection. But there was always the chance that one of these flares might fall, still glowing, at your feet, or right on to you, if you were on the ground.

By dawn everyone would have returned to the trenches and the order "STAND TO (ARMS)" would be given. Then every man had to be alert with rifle loaded and bayonet fixed. As dawn broke the periscope watch of 'No-man's land' was resumed. To keep eyes and senses alert after days and nights with practically no sleep strained will power to the limit, but to be caught asleep at "STAND TO" was a very serious offence which could result in court martial. However, the arrival of a cup of tea laced with rum at "STAND DOWN" served as a reviver. Stew (skilly) and tea would be fetched up by the orderly men for the day from the field cookers located just behind the lines. These supplies were transported in large cylinders which had an outer annular space filled with hot water. This device was suppose to keep the inner, consumable contents warm. As can be imagined, by the time the orderlies had struggled along communication trenches which were often deep in mud, the containers hot fare was no longer very hot.

It was not possible to remove or change any item of clothing while in the trenches. There were no facilities for ablutions, and elementary arrangements to serve as latrines were usually excavated out of the side of the trench. In such mole-like conditions uniforms, even in spells of dry weather, soon became soiled, and in wet weather, caked in mud. It can hardly be surprising then that a missile causing the simplest injury could carry dirt into the wound and the threat of of gangrene. In the heavily manured soil of Belgium this was to cause a condition previously unknown to the medical profession, *gas gangrene*. Evacuating the wounded from the front line was another problem, the trenches often being too narrow to allow a stretcher to be manoeuvred around the corners of the bays, etc. A wounded man would therefore be made as comfortable as possible on a stretcher in a dug-out or rough shelter cut into the side of the trench until he could be carried out *over the top* after dark. In the meantime he would be given First Aid, using the field dressing sewn into the lower right flap of his tunic. This consisted of a waterproof cover containing a phial of iodine, which would first be poured into the wound, and a two and a half yard bandage with a gauze pad stitched eighteen inches from one end, with which to cover the wound. Only a reader old enough to have had a cut or graze painted with iodine will be able to imagine the effect of a phial of iodine being poured into an open and, probably deep, wound. Less seriously wounded men who were mobile would have their wounds dressed, and be told to make their own way back to the line as *Walking wounded*. However, it was not unknown for apparently *lightly* wounded men, making their own way to a Casualty Clearing Station, to suddenly fall down dead. We now know that these men had died of shock caused by their wounds.

These conditions led to another landmark of which everyone soon became aware. This was the discovery of body lice in underwear. It should be explained that spare underwear, except socks, was not included in a soldier's kit. It is well to remember that a soldier carried everything he owned on his back when he moved. Exchange underwear was supplied from a common stock of used garments which, after the indescribably squalid conditions of the trenches, would all have been infested with body lice. These exchange garments would be issued, supposedly cleaned and fumigated, when soldiers came out of the line to rest. However, once donned, the heat of the body would hatch the eggs in the seams, and the itching would return.

The men were soon able to identify the sound and results of the more common types of projectile. *Whizzbangs*, small, low trajectory, high velocity shells, were most likely to be aimed at forward positions. High trajectory *5.9's* usually were used to knock out mine heads and trench mortar positions. *Minenwerfers* or *Minnies, were* enormous 110 lbs cigar-shaped mortar bombs, standing 3 foot 6 inches, which gave a 'pop' as they left the mortar. The *Minnie* was the largest projectile of its kind used by the German Army. They were said to wobble their way across No-man's land making a distinctive "Whoosh, Whoosh" sound whilst airborne, and on such an uncertain trajectory that the recipients were never sure where the projectile would land. It was said, however, that a few yards either way was no matter, so enormous was the destruction it caused. Men caught by this weapon simply disappeared. It was often necessary to parade a platoon to establish who had been killed. Rifle grenades were a particularly nasty device which, giving no warning of their approach, simply 'arrived' on the parapet. These were about the size of a Mills grenade. Snipers in *Hides* in No-Man's Land would fire with great accuracy at anything which moved above the parapet, so "Keeping your head down" was literally a matter of life or death.

The 16th Battalion suffered its first casualty on April 22nd, when Private E. MacKay, the C.O.'s servant, was seriously wounded by a whizz-bang splinter. The following day Privates Smith, Slingsby and Bannister, all of 'C' Company, were killed by shell fire. They were buried that night near Sucrerie. On June 4th, shell fire blew in 'C' Company Headquarters, killing Lieutenant R. E. Laxton and burying Captain Russel, who subsequently died.

One morning at daybreak in early June a large notice appeared in front of the German line, somewhere near Redan. It read:

HAMPSHIRE SUNK
KITCHENER DEAD

On his first day in the front line, George Morgan found himself on duty in a 'listening post' some way in front of his own parapet. A listening post may have been a "sap head" reached via a narrow trench dug out from the front line, but, more usually, was an isolated shell hole, heavily wired in. Their purpose was to provide early warning of enemy activity. He later admitted to being more afraid of the huge brown rats that thrived on the dead in No-mans land, than he was of the Germans. Later, while he slept in a dug-out, one of these foul scavengers ate its way through the side of his haversack to steal his cheese ration. He never lost his loathing of these creatures and, in later months, waged a personal war against them. His ploy was to fix a piece of cheese to the tip of his bayonet. He would then place his rifle across the parapet, his finger on the trigger, taking up the first pressure. The first rat to nibble at his cheese promptly received a round of ball and was despatched to its "happy hunting ground".

George Morgan, the young recruit

George well remembered his feelings on their first relief from trench duty. They were met a short distance behind the line by the Battalion cooks with field cookers, brought up as near as they dared. He huddled up to the side of a field cooker, enjoying its radiated heat, sipped strong hot tea which tasted of wood smoke, munched a cold thick bacon sandwich in thick slices of bread, and listened to the dull, ever-present, rumble of artillery which was to form the backdrop to his life for the next two years. His feelings were a combination of relief and just a little self satisfaction. Had he not survived, passed his own, self-set test? Perhaps it would not be so bad, after all.

One of the differences the *Pals* experienced in France was the much harsher application of the British Army disciplinary code compared with their earlier experiences in the Middle East. For example, it is said that Field-Marshal Haig considered an occasional execution by firing squad of anyone who could be accused of cowardice or desertion to be 'good for discipline'. This was brought home to the *Pals* at an early date when two young soldiers from one of the battalions, out on an evening spree in a local *estaminet,* drank rather too much wine and, as a result, were unable to find their way back to their camp. They were picked up by the Military Police and subsequently brought before a Court Martial charged with being absent from their place of duty while on active service. The Court found them guilty and sentenced them to Death by Firing Squad. Everyone in their Battalion was convinced that they would be reprieved. The punishment for the offence when in England would have been ten days confined to barracks and, after all, this was an all volunteer battalion - desertion was unthinkable. However, this was not to be. The Battalion was confined to camp for two days, after which they were paraded and told of the Court's finding, of the sentence and that "the sentence has been duly carried out." One thousand young volunteers stood on parade in a bewildered silence.

The families of these two unfortunate young Bradfordians were advised that the two had been *killed in action.* It was the wish of the members of the Bradford Pals Old Comrades' Association, who told the writer this story in 1976, that any surviving next of kin should be allowed to continue to believe that this was how those two young men met their deaths. I am sure that all who read this book will want the wishes of those *Old Pals* to be honoured.

Mr Cyril Tetlow, who lived in Heaton until his death in 1961 and who served with the 21st Battalion, West Yorkshire Regiment, once recalled how, whilst working as a clerk in his company office, he took notes from the Company Sergeant Major on the items required for a forthcoming execution which his battalion had been selected to carry out. The C.S.M. listed the following items:

1. A wooden chair to sit the condemned on.

2. Sandbags with which to weigh down the chair so as to prevent the condemned kicking it over in a bid to save himself.

3. Sufficient rope to tie the arms and legs of the condemned to the chair.

4. A hood-type gas helmet to put over the head of the condemned (put on backwards so that the eye pieces were at the rear).

5. A disc of white paper or cloth of about six inches diameter, together with a pin to fix to the tunic over the heart of the condemned as an aiming point.

6. A firing squad of twelve men would need to be selected. They would be handed previously loaded rifles, a proportion of which would be loaded with blank cartridges.

7. A suitable spot would need to be selected for the execution.

Cyril Tetlow also recalled another occasion when, visiting a local *estaminet* to enjoy the luxury of a plate of egg and chips, he met a friend from civilian life who was serving with another battalion. His friend, normally abstemious, ordered a large brandy and, ashen faced and visibly shaken, said to him: "This morning I was on a firing party, we shot a lad from another battalion. I feel terrible."

During the First World War some 346 British soldiers were executed for desertion or cowardice, 10% of them officers, although ten times that number were sentenced to death but had their sentences commuted. Battle fatigue was recognised as a sickness by the Americans long before the British.

One family who discovered the fate of their son, Private A. Ingham of the Manchester Regiment, a boy of seventeen who was charged with deserting a front line trench, had his gravestone inscribed:

SHOT AT DAWN
ONE OF THE FIRST TO ENLIST
A WORTHY SON OF HIS FATHER

When Mr Bill Hughes, the then Prime Minister of Australia, heard of this incentive for good discipline he warned the Field-Marshal that if he allowed the execution of just one Australian soldier then the ANZACs would be removed from his command. It is interesting to note that, in two world wars,

31st Division men moving into the front line in 1916. *Imperial War Museum, Negative Q 10611.*

Australian and New Zealand soldiers proved to be some of the most ferocious shock troops in the allied armies, even without the Field-Marshal's incentive.

The whole brigade moved to Gezaincourt on June 19th. Here they began a special course of training to prepare them for the coming offensive. Here they practised *going over the top,* leaving trenches by way of assault ladders, the principle of attacking in *wave formations,* that is advancing in open order while maintaining spacing and direction and attacking their objectives - trenches dug to represent those of the enemy.

When their training was complete they were addressed by the Corps Commander, Lieutenant-General Sir A. G. Hunter-Weston, who was not liked by the *Pals* because of, in their view, his superior attitude, and known by them as 'Bunter-Weston'. He told them that, having watched them in training, he was delighted with all he had seen, that all they would have to do was "walk into Serre" as all the Germans would be dead, a view which they were not inclined to share. This was to be the *Big Push* which would end the war. Reserves of men, including the Cavalry Divisions, were waiting to stream through the gap they were to make in the German lines, etc., etc. This was to be, for the *Pals,* a marvellous chance to finish the war.

They were told that "even if your brother or your friend falls wounded, do not stop for him. He will be tended to by the stretcher bearers."

They were also told that there would be so-called *Battle Police* in the trenches and armed with revolvers, who would shoot dead anyone who refused to 'go over the top'. They were bewildered by this, even angry. At that date, June 30th 1916, the strength of the British Army in France was 1,426,000 men, *all of whom were volunteers*.

While at Gezaincourt Major G. S. Guyon of the Royal Fusiliers arrived to command the 16th Battalion.

This photograph gives some impression of the extent of the barbed wire in No-man's land. *Imperial War Museum, Negative E 3583.*

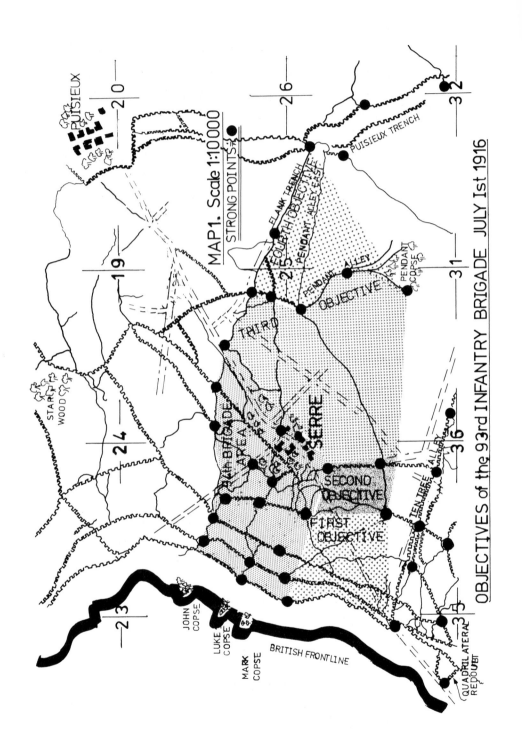

MAP1. Scale 1:10000

STRONG POINTS

OBJECTIVES of the 93rd INFANTRY BRIGADE JULY 1st 1916

PUISIEUX

PUISIEUX TRENCH

FLANK TRENCH

FOURTH OBJECTIVE

PENDANT ALLEY EAST

PENDANT ALLEY

THIRD OBJECTIVE

PENDANT COPSE

SERRE

94th BRIGADE AREA

SECOND OBJECTIVE

FIRST OBJECTIVE

TEN TREE ALLEY

STARCH WOOD

JOHN COPSE

LUKE COPSE

MARK COPSE

BRITISH FRONTLINE

QUADRILATERAL REDOUBT

A battalion of the 31st Division marching to the front line before the attack on July 1st, 1916. *Imperial War Museum, Negative Q 743.*

CHAPTER 3: THE SOMME

"Good morning, good morning," the General said
When we met him last week on our way to the line.
Now the soldiers he smiled at are most of 'em dead,
And we're cursing his staff for incompetent swine.
"He's a cheery old card," grunted Harry to Jack
As they slogged up to Arras with rifle and pack.

. . . .
But he did for them both with his plan of attack.
Siegfried Sassoon

The valley of the Somme at the end of June was the place and time selected by General Joffre and Field-Marshal Douglas Haig for their combined offensive of 1916. Their objectives were threefold:

1: To relieve the pressure on Verdun;
2: To assist the Allies in other theatres of the war by stopping the transfer of any enemy troops from the western front;
3: To wear down the strength of the enemy forces facing them.

It is beyond the scope of this book to attempt an analysis of the execution of this plan. Let the words of Sir Winston Churchill in his book 'World Crises' suffice:

The military conceptions underlaying the scheme of attack were characterised by simplicity. The policy of the French and British commanders had selected, as a point for their offensive, what was undoubtably the strongest and most perfectly defended position in the world.

The 31st Division formed part of Lieutenant-General Sir A.G. Hunter-Weston's VIII Corps on the British left. The role allocated to the Division in the assault was to attack on a 'two-brigade' front, with the 94th Brigade on the left and the 93rd Brigade on the right, take Serre and then swing left, thus closing the left flank and protecting the advance of the 4th and 29th Divisions, fighting on their right.

Each brigade was to attack on a 'two company front', that is each battalion advancing in two waves, each of two companies. The 92nd Brigade formed the divisional reserve.

The 93rd Infantry Brigade was to complete its task in four 'bounds'. The troops in each 'bound' were to hold the ground they had taken, whilst the troops in the next 'bound' leap-frogged through them.

First Bound:

The object of the first bound for the 93rd Brigade was the German trench K30c 2.6 to the junction of the trenches at K36a 1.9. This trench was to be taken by the 15th West Yorkshire Regiment (the 'Leeds Pals') and then consolidated and garrisoned by two companies of that battalion. The line was to be known as the GREEN LINE.

The Second Bound:

The 16th West Yorks were to leap-frog through the GREEN LINE and take the German trenches K36a 8.7. This was to be consolidated and garrisoned by the two remaining companies of the 15th West Yorks and was to be known as the RED LINE.

The Third Bound:

The objective of this bound was to be the German trench running from the South East corner of the orchard at L23a 2.6 to L25a 7.4 and then to Pendant Copse. This line was to be taken by the 16th Battalion with one company of the Durham

Light Infantry on their right. This line was to be consolidated and garrisoned by the 16th Battalion together with their Durham Light Infantry comrades and was to be known as the BROWN LINE.

The Fourth Bound:

The fourth and final objective was to take the German trench from point L25a 7.4 to the crossroads at L26a 5.6 and thence the junction of Pendant Alley East and Puiseux trench. This task was allocated to the 18th Battalion, who were also to consolidate and garrison it, and was to be known as the BLUE LINE. This final bound would have swung the line left and sealed the flank, the British now occupying a line running from John Copse to Puisieux trench.

The actual attack on each line was to be carried out by waves of troops at distances from fifty to two hundred yards apart. The confidence which the staff planners placed in the effectiveness of the five-day bombardment of the German lines which preceded the assault is reflected by the stores and equipment which the battle order required to be carried by troops completing each 'bound forward'. These were as follows:

By all N.C.O.'s and other ranks:
> Waterproof sheet and cardigan
> 3 sandbags
> 170 rounds small arms ammunition
> Full water bottle
> I extra day's rations
> 2 mills bombs

By all men:
> 1 pick or shovel in the proportion of 2 shovels to 1 pick.

Added to this, of course, was a rifle, with fully charged magazine, and bayonet weighing about 10 lbs. Gas masks were to be carried by all ranks. In addition the brigade battle order required that wire cutters should be carried by each section according to the number available. These were attached by a lanyard to the shoulder strap and carried in the belt. Men carrying wire cutters were required to wear a yellow arm band, this apparently to facilitate the salvaging of cutters from the dead. Two mallets were required to be carried in a similar manner by each platoon and to be used in the removal of enemy wire entanglements in order to 'use them for our own purposes'.Each platoon was also required to carry six rolls of barbed wire, each roll being carried on stakes between two men. The total load carried by each man was probably in the order of 90 lbs.

With the foregoing in mind the battle order instructions under the heading of DISCIPLINE is most illuminating, and reads:

"When advancing to the attack, cheering and doubling should not be allowed. The former advertises the fact that troops are attacking and the latter is too great an effort to men carrying heavy weights."

One of the lessons learnt by the British Army at the Battle of Loos the previous year was that German snipers were trained to select as priority targets British officers, easily identified by their distinctive tunics with 'Sam Brown' belts, riding breeches and brown boots. As a result, casualties among officers had been high. Therefore officers were instructed to dress "as nearly as possible like their men. Puttees must be worn, if necessary over their trench boots. Badges of rank will be worn on the shoulder straps, not on the sleeve." However this order was ignored by most officers, one of whom carried only a walking stick when he 'went over the top', which may account for the repeated experience of high casualties amongst the officers.

During the preliminary bombardment of the enemy front, one which began on June 25th, a lull was arranged each night at varying times to allow British patrols to examine the enemy's wire. On the night of June 29th at approximately 11.30 p.m. Lieutenant Clough of the 18th Battalion led a fighting patrol, consisting of four officers and 25 other ranks, towards the German front. However, when some 25 yards from the enemy line, they came under a heavy bomb attack and suffered heavy casualties.

Two officers and nine other ranks were killed and 18 other ranks wounded, two of whom later died of their wounds. Lieutenant Clough, himself wounded, reported the enemy trenches to be deep and well manned.

His report reads as follows:

"Party left our front line trenches as scheduled 12.28 p.m., 30th June, 1916. Advance was slow owing to numerous shell holes and flares. Apparently our party was seen as soon as we had left our own trenches for they seemed prepared for us and we were met by bombs when between 25 and 30 yards from their trenches. They sent up a single green rocket and formed a barrage of hand grenades in front of us and trench mortars and artillery behind us. The trenches seemed fairly knocked about and the wire was cut, where we were, in sufficient quantity to allow the passage of troops. Their trenches seemed very full of men and apparently are very deep.

Finding we could not get forward, I brought my party back as well and as soon as I possibly could. This took some two hours. As far as I can judge, my casualties at present are about ten killed and 12 wounded, out of 38 men and four officers. At present two officers, Lieutenant F. Watson and 2nd Lieutenant J. W. Worsnop, are missing. I have been slightly wounded myself in two places. Our H. E. shells were all dropping a little over half way between our line and the German line and quite 20 yards short of their wire, and this was taking place during our scheduled hour for the raid. My watch, sent by Colonel Craven, was synchronized with our artillery officers."

Other patrols on VIII Corps front were reporting 'not much damage to wire' and 'not a sign of a gap anywhere'. Whether the General Staff disbelieved these reports or merely chose to ignore them, sticking to their belief that 'no one could remain alive after this, the heaviest bombardment in history' it is not possible to say.

After a meeting with Lieutenant-General Sir A. G. Hunter-Weston, the Brigadier Major wrote, "The Corps Commander was extremely optimistic, telling everyone that the wire had been blown away, although we could see it standing strong and well: that there would be no German trenches and all we had to do was walk into Serre". Nevertheless General Sir Henry Rawlinson, commanding the Fourth Army, wrote in his diary on the evening of June 30th: " . . . the artillery work during the bombardment and the wire cutting had been done well, except in VIII Corps which is somewhat behind."

On June 30th, both battalions received instructions to move up to the trenches that night. Most ranks spent the afternoon writing letters and 'putting one's affairs in order'. Sergeant H. Drake was to remember a friend who spent the time writing a lengthy and detailed will. His friend was shot through the head while climbing over the parapet a few hours later. In a letter which later appeared in the *Bradford Daily Mail*, Lieutenant R. Sutcliff wrote: "Just a line to say I go 'over the lid' tomorrow. My company are in the first line of attack and hope to do great things. Naturally we hope to come through alright but someone's bound to go under and it's the only way to end the war. It's a great thing to be in and I'm glad our division is one of the first chosen to go over."

George Morgan spent the afternoon with his friends, Billy Booth, Bill Kenny and Dawson Horne. Bill Kenny expressed the view that "in this attack some of us are going to be killed." He asked George to exchange home addresses with him and to agree that, should one of them not survive, then the other would write to next of kin.

A reserve of 10% of all ranks was selected to remain behind to form the nucleus of new battalions, should casualties prove heavy. In the early evening the battalions marched out of Bus-les-Artois, moving off in half companies, the 16th Battalion at 6.35 p.m. and the 18th Battalion at 8.45 p.m., and made towards the sound of the guns. A sound which had been heard distinctly at a distance of 12 miles for the last five days. As they marched out of the village they passed on the roadside their Divisional Commander, Major General R. Wanless O'Gowan and some of his staff sitting astride beautifully groomed horses. He called out: "Good luck, men, there is not a German left in their trenches. Our guns have blown them to Hell!" They marched with a great clatter of studded boots on the pave, weapons and equipment jangling and rattling. After watching his comrades swing past, whistling and singing, full of youthful confidence, Fred Rawlings, who stayed behind with the 16th Battalion's reserve, wrote in his diary: "Battalion set off in good spirits. Wish I was going with them."

In an orchard a little to the north west of Colin Camps, they ate a meal of bully beef stew and then, at 10.00 p.m., moved on. As they passed through Colin Camps the villagers lined the street and stood insilent salute as their allies marched by, even though the village was subjected to shelling, being only two kilometres behind the line. It was here that the 18th Battalion suffered their first casualty, Captain Duckitt of 'D' Company, who was wounded by a shell

Captain C. S. Duckitt

splinter. Cross country tracks, marked by tapes led them to the communication trenches, Southern Avenue and Sackville Street, and thence to the assembly trenches (see map 2). Men glanced in awe towards the barrage which thundered and flashed in the eastern sky. As they approached the forward trenches the sense of comradeship seemed to grow stronger. Behind Sackville Street, conveniently near the casualty clearing station in Basin Wood, the pioneer Battalion, the 12th King's Own Yorkshire Light Infantry, had dug a large common grave around which there already lay a number of blanket draped bodies, evidence of the pounding the 92nd Brigade had been receiving whilst holding the line. This was underlined as they entered the communication trench where their progress was repeatedly halted by the difficuties faced by stretcher bearers having to manoeuvre their loads around the incoming troops.

Both battalions were now taking casualties from shell fire. It was in Sackville Street that George Morgan's cousin, Sergeant Bill Morgan, was killed, his head shattered by a shell splinter. Word reached George Morgan, "Billy Morgan's got it" but there was no time for sentiment in the war and George had to go on. Sergeant Morgan had been in the battalion from the beginning, his battalion number was "8".

Private Dawson Horne

By 3.00 a.m. all companies were in the position allocated.'A' and 'C' Companies of the 16th Battalion, together with the Company of the Durham Light Infantry, occupied North and South Monk trenches whilst the remaining two companies were situated in Bradford trench, 'B' Company on the right and 'D' Company on the left. The two leading Companies of the 18th Battalion 'A' and 'D' occupied Dunmow trench, whilst 'C' and 'B' Companies assembled in Languard trench.

It was a clear starlit night, the main hostile activity seemingly being indicated by the drone of shells passing overhead in both directions. Putting his spade across the trench George Morgan formed a makeshift seat. Carefully he applied his weight and, finding it hold, leaned his back against the trench wall, grateful for a chance to rest his aching limbs. Looking around his new surroundings his eyes fell on the corpse of a young soldier, probably killed by a shell burst. Thrown on to the parados, a hand hung back into the trench, the fingers clawed in final agony, the head lolled back, the jaw sagged in a stupid expression, the sightless eyes stared at the night sky. In his mind's eye George saw a small child looking up into the face of a young woman, asking: "Does everyone die, Mummy?"
"Yes, they do," replied the young woman.
"Will I die, Mummy?"
"Yes," replied the young woman, "but not for a long time."

Everyone was too keyed up to sleep but there was very little talking now, everyone sat alone with his own thoughts, thinking of home and family. Apprehension must have played its part, too, but George remembered being more afraid of showing his fear and 'letting the side down'. The one exception was Dawson

Sappers installing assault ladders in assembly trench. *Imperial War Museum.Negative Q 6229.*

Horne who, even at that hour, never lost his cheerfulness and his ability to make a joke. He called to George "When we get into the German trenches, if I can find a little German without his rifle, won't I chase the bugger round!!"

Whilst they awaited zero hour, all ranks received an issue of rum. The men in George Morgan's section registered their disgust when Captain Smith, who commanded 'B' Company and a strict teetotaller, poured the surplus down a sump hole. Dawson Horne refused his ration, saying, "I prefer to 'go over' right in the head." George Morgan was to be the third man to go up his particular assault ladder; as they waited for zero hour with hearts thumping, stomachs twisting into knots, mouths dry, he could still hear the voice of Dawson Horne, joking, "I can't wait to get at 'em."

As Dick Collins waited with Dickie Bond, the Bradford City international outside right, to go over the top together as part of a Lewis gun section of four men, he was hit on the back by a spent shrapnel ball. Dickie Bond said to him, "You've got yours. You won't get another now", but Dickie Bond was to be proved wrong.

The men were told that 'battle police' had been ordered to shoot anyone who refused to leave the trench at zero hour. George Morgan remembered the anger of the men of the all-volunteer battalion at such a suggestion, and the words just quoted of Dawson Horne, which were to prove the last he ever heard from his friend.

On the opposite side of No-man's land, knee high with summer grass, awaited the highly professional and battle hardened troops of the 169th Regiment. Crouched in their deep shelters, they waited for the barrage to lift. This, they knew, would be the moment to haul machine guns and ammunition up dug-out steps and into position.

At 6.25am the bombardment, by 18 pounders, 4.5 inch Howitzers and 2 inch trench mortars concentrated its attention upon the enemy front line and forward assembly trenches. The enemy artillery replied, bombarding the crowded assembly trenches with shrapnel. At 7.10am, the British bombardment lifted off the enemy front line. Ten minutes later an intense bombardment of the German trenches by light trench mortars began. German artillery retaliated with equal intensity bringing down a deluge of explosive on the British positions.

At 7.21am the leading platoons of the 15th Battalion (the 'Leeds Pals') went over the parapet and lined previously laid tapes. Immediately enemy machine guns began firing at them and German troops were seen lining and firing from their parapet. Private R. N. Bell of "B" Company recalled:

"As daylight came with the promise of a fine and warm day and as the hours passed, the enemy turned his attention to the front line trenches on which shrapnel shells and whizz-bangs were now being directed all along the front line leaving us with no doubt about the awareness of the Germans of the imminence of the coming attack. As zero hour drew near the hail of shellbursts overhead and on the front line, where volumes of earth were being thrown up, seemed to increase and the noise was such as to mask the sound of our own artillery. As regards the intended contribution by the Stokes trench mortars operating in or near our own front line in the final stage, there is no knowing whether it had any effect. On the other hand, to quote the official history of the war, the enemy barrage on our lines at this point was described *as so constant and severe that the cones of the explosions gave the impression of a thick belt of poplar trees.*

Just before 7.30 came the shrill sound of the platoon officers' whistles signalling the order to rise from the trenches and move forward. For a fleeting moment this seemed almost welcome but, almost simultaneously with the sound of the whistles, a new sound joined the din from shell fire, and that was the rattle of machine gun fire directly on our front, soon to be joined by others, the significance of which could not have been lost to any of us. Despite all this those still unwounded scrambled out of the Assembly trench, dug a short distance behind the front line, as best they could, "A" Company into no-man's land and "B" Company a short distance behind. For my part, almost immediately on reaching the surface, my foot caught on a projecting piece of wire and I sprawled full length on the ground. Picking myself up I moved forward with the rest, that is those who had not already been hit, until we were able to drop into the shell torn front line. In front of me at this time was my platoon commander on the point of climbing out again from the fire step, when he fell back having been hit in the face. At the same time a call came from the right to 'move to the left', as the well-known figure of the Grenadier Guards Sergeant, attached to the Battalion since its formation, his face now covered with blood, appeared from the right moving towards me. The trench was now almost blocked with dead and wounded, all of whom I knew well and had served with for over a year. Having made my way a little further along leftwards, as instructed, I realised that I was entirely alone, the rest of the company seemingly having melted away and, although a momentary glance to the rear had shown waves of man in open order - the 16th Battalion West Yorks., presumably - nothing more was seen of them. All this took place in less time than it takes to write about and the parapet was still being swept by machine gun fire."

Private Bell remembered that, later in the day when survivors of the battalion assembled in a support trench, only 49 uninjured men answered a roll call.

The 15th Battalion had lost all its officers almost at once. Eleven were killed and eleven were wounded, including their Commanding Officer, Major R. B. Neill, who was wounded, and the Adjutant, Captain Stanley T. A. Neil, who was killed. Of those who left the front line trench, few advanced more than a hundred yards beyond the British wire. Of those who left Leeds trench in the second wave, few advanced more than forty yards from the parapet.

At 7.30am in response to the shrill call of officers' whistles, the leading platoons of the 16th Battalion's, 'A' and 'C' Companies and 'D' Company of the 18th Durhams, climbed out of North and South Monk trenches. They stepped into a nightmare of exploding shells and machine gun fire. To help maintain direction everyone had been instructed to 'make straight for Serre Church steeple'. The fact that five days of heavy bombardment would probably have reduced the church to a heap of rubble, as indeed it had, seems to have escaped the attention of the planners. By the time they had advanced as far as Leeds trench they had suffered heavily. By 8.35am most of the Officers, including the Commanding Officer, Major Guyon, were killed or wounded, and the advance was held up. Let 2nd Lieutenant C.F.Laxton, the Battalion Intelligence Officer, take up the story:

"...at five minutes to zero Major Guyon, Ransome and myself left our headquarters for the front line. We had only been in SAP. A about two minutes when Major Guyon was struck through the helmet by a bullet. Ransome and I were alongside at the time, and bandaged him up, though unconscious and apparently dying, the wound being in the temple. We were obliged to leave as things did not appear to be going well. We urged the men on, and saw the columns advancing over Leeds trench, one being led by Captain Pringle. Things seemed to stop, men were falling and no one advancing over our front line. Stead was in the front line with a few men, which we scraped together for a rush. Stead and I scrambled out and the men tried to follow, but were mown down by machine gun fire, I got about 15 yards before being hit by a bullet in the left knee and a piece of shrapnel in the right thigh and managed to crawl to a shell hole about 5 yards in front, where I found Stead shot dead. After staying there for about 15 minutes, I tried to regain our trenches, leaving all surplus kit, and gained a shell hole a few yards nearer. Ransome evidently saw me and came out to my assistance. I sent him back to find the nearest place where I could crawl into the trench, this he did and I followed him. This was the last I saw of him but afterwards I heard he was suffering from shell shock with Lieutenant Hoffman."

Private Harry Severn of "A" Company had hardly stepped off the parapet when he was struck by fragments from a German shell which exploded close by. He lay on the ground for some time, in great pain, passing in and out of consciousness with his right arm shattered and his left arm also badly injured. Some time after dusk he heard a stretcher bearer say "don't bother with him, he's had it." Determined to prove them wrong, willing himself back into consciousness, he somehow got to his feet and staggered, crawled and dragged himself back to the relative safety of the trench which he had recently left. From there he was taken to a Casualty Clearing Station.

In a letter to his parents Private George Gransbury of the 16th Battalion wrote:

"Over we went and, as we were the first the fireworks started. The Bosche meant keeping us at long range, and, not caring to be gun fodder, we knocked on and got about 100 yards, and only about 25 of us left in our Company. Our officer was wounded and a corporal was in charge. Still, on we went and began to miss each other. I dropped on Captain Pringle, who was wounded, and dragged him to a shell hole in which were Captain D. Smith (wounded in the back), and Lieutenant R. Sutcliffe, also wounded. A few privates filled up the spare places. I was creeping up the side of the crater to see what was going on when a high explosive dropped right on top of us. How I escaped, God alone knows. Captain Pringle was blown from the opposite side on to the top of me and I was buried but could breathe. A lad came along and helped me out."

As the first platoons of 'B' and 'D' Companies clambered over the parapet of Bradford trench, they too came under a heavy fire from high explosives, shrapnel and machine guns. 'B' Company began to take casualties, although 'D' Company did not suffer heavily until they came up to, and over, the front line. Heavy machine gun fire then took a dreadful toll.

Number 7 platoon, 'B' Company, was led 'over the lid' by 2nd Lieutenant Simms, a debonair young man fresh from public school. He sprang up the assault ladder and over the parapet, calling to his men to follow him. He was very calm and smoking a cigarette, revolver in hand, in the best traditions of a British Officer. His men clambered out after him, although George Morgan nearly fell backwards off the assault ladder, such was the weight of his equipment. As he stepped over the parapet he was almost knocked back into the trench by Private Norman Illingworth, his hands covering his face, blood streaming through his fingers, who blundered into him, and then fell headlong into the trench. As he lined up on the starting tape, a ruddy complexioned man to his left, who had only recently arrived in a draft from England, screamed, fell against him and crumpled up - his complexion drained to chalk as his life blood spilled out. Over on his right a man, hit in the crutch, was writhing on the ground, clutching his wound, screaming in agony. Looking half towards the left he could see the village of Puisieux blazing, set alight by British shelling.

They moved off from the starting tape as if on parade, rifles held at the port. After a few paces his friend, Billy Booth, fell badly wounded, crying out "Oh God! Help me, do help me". Corporal Harry Metcalf called out: 'Leave him, George, we must go on. He'll be seen to by the stretcher bearers". Another few paces and Harry Metcalf was hit and fell, calling out: "Go on, George, the second wave will be along any minute". George was now completely alone, his section having melted away. A shell splinter sliced off one of his ammunition pouches and knocked him on to his back. Deciding that he 'could not fight the war alone' he took shelter in a shell hole to await the next wave, the 18th Battalion, intending to go on with them, but the 18th Battalion never reached him. He was, in fact, the only member of his section to survive the battle unhurt. Some time later he was able to regain Bradford trench where he stumbled over the body of Private Norman Waudilove, only son of the Bradford industrialist. He had been shot dead whilst climbing the assault ladder and had fallen back into the trench. Death must have been instantaneous, he looked as if he had fallen asleep. Near the parapet he saw the body of Corporal Squire Clough. His back had been torn open by wounds so numerous that it was impossible to estimate their number.

Corporal Squire Clough

Many of those who witnessed the assault could not initially understand why so many of the advancing men were doubling up and falling onto their knees in such odd postures. It was only when they became able to distinguish the screams of the wounded above the noise of battle that they realised these men had been hit.

Sergeant Major G. Cussons, who left Bradford trench with 'B' Company headquarters, is recorded as saying:

"at 7.25, five minutes before zero, the enemy machine guns, rifle fire and shrapnel were directed against the parapet of our assembly trench, the southern half of Bradford trench, causing us to suffer considerably. A lot of men never got off the ladder but fell back from the parapet. On getting out of the trenches to take up our positions in front, we lost heavily through the line to shrapnel, machine gun and rapid rifle fire. By the time we attained our position in front of Bradford trench most of the Officers and N.C.O.'s and many men had been knocked out. At zero we advanced and continued to advance until the company head-quarters with which I was, found ourselves in front of the battalion - all in front having been hit. We found ourselves then half way between Leeds trench and the front line. At this point I continued to advance, Captain D. Smith having been knocked out. (Captain Smith's last message to 'Battalion,' brought in. by his runner, read 'Company advancing steadily') and I carried on until I reached the front line.

In our advance we passed the majority of 'A' Company, laying killed or wounded, halfway between Leeds trench and the front line. I found in the front line a good many men of the 15th Battalion West Yorks and what was left of the Durham Light Infantry Company who were attached to us. Also a few of the King's Own Yorkshire Light Infantry. I found no Officers or N.C.O.'s of these Regiments or of my own Regiment. The order came to 'ease off to the left'. I proceeded to do this and found Lieutenant Jowett of my Regiment, who ordered me to try to collect and organise the few men who were left with a view to advancing again. At this moment the enemy started shelling our front line very heavily, with shrapnel and high explosives. This would be nearly one hour after zero, but of course I cannot give the correct time. Within a very short time, all the men we had collected were knocked out including Mr. Jowett, who gave me instructions to make my way back to Battalion Headquarters and report that there were no men left. He told me that he had already sent back to Battalion Headquarters three or four times but without success. This would be about one hour and a half after zero, and I could make out that some of our men were then advancing towards the enemy lines and must have been quite close up to the German parapet. I saw some of the Germans show themselves over the parapet, shoot at and throw bombs at what must have been some of our men who were still advancing."

The last message received from 'D' Company, brought in by Private Drake, the company runner, read:

TO: O/C 16th West Yorks
FROM: O/C 'D' Company
            'D' Company advancing. Casualties unknown.
            (Sgd.) Alan Clough, Captain
PLACE: In front of Bradford trench
TIME: 8.00 a.m., 1.7.16

Private Price (Machine Gun Section) whose gun was carried behind the last line (the last platoon) with orders to follow up 'D' Company, later recorded:

> "....my own section was wiped out as we went into No-man's-land. We were 70 yards out and I saw Captain Clough on our left and further left our other gun. We went out and over the parapet at a slow double. Met a man of the 15th West Yorks, he said that no one had passed him advancing - the rest dropped through travasing machine gun fire. I looked at the front line but could see no Germans. We stayed there for some time - until about 2.00 p.m. In the meantime my No. 1 had crawled back (I hear he is still alive). I crawled out and got into Sackville trench and finally reported to Battalion Headquarters. I saw Captain Clough wounded in No-man's land, probably in the left wrist, he appeared to try to move backwards and I think he was hit again. Of the machine gun section to which I was attached, five of the six got into No man's-land before being hit."

At 8.20 am the 18th Battalion Headquarters received a message from 'Brigade' that the 16th Battalion was held up and ordering the commanding officer to go forward to SAP "A" to investigate. Having assessed the situation the Colonel rejoined his leading companies in Dunmow trench. Here Private Frank Hartley said to him: "You're not wearing your identity discs, Sir." The Colonel smiled and replied: "I shan't need them."

As the order 'fix bayonets' rang out among the waiting companies of the 18th Battalion, Corporal Norman Goldthorpe's Platoon Commander, Lieutenant Foizey, turned to him and said "I shan't come back." Corporal Goldthorpe told him to believe he would as "I certainly believe I shall. " However, his premonition was to prove correct. At 8.40am they began to leave their trenches. The first wave, 'A' and 'D' Companies from Dunmow trench', 'C' and 'B' Companies from Languard trench. These positions had been subjected to a heavy bombardment of high explosives and shrapnel since some fifteen minutes before zero. As Ernest Wilson clambered over the parapet he saw the Adjutant, Captain F. T. Williams, who had climbed out in front of him, thrown 20 feet into the air by a shell burst. He advanced a few paces and was himself struck down by a shrapnel ball. Captain C. H. C. Keen who commanded 'A' Company fell, seriously wounded, almost as soon as he left the parapet. Frank Burn described the scene as 'a hell on earth'.

Less than a hundred yards in front of Dunmow trench they came under a heavy cross fire from machine guns firing from their right, probably from the Quadrilateral Redoubt and south of the Serre Road. Almost everyone dropped flat on their stomachs to escape this murderous scythe, except their commanding Officer, Lieutenant-Colonel M. N. Kennard. Standing calm and erect amid the crack and whine of bullets and carrying only a walking stick he called out "come on boys, up you get," turned and began to walk at an easy gait towards the enemy. The battalion rose to their feet and followed him. As they came out of the dead ground in which their assembly trenches were dug they were additionally engaged by a rapid rifle fire from the front. Casualties were heavy, particularly amongst the officers and including Lieutenant-Colonel Kennard, who was killed by a shell which burst close by him.

Lieutenant R. S. Cross who commanded No. 4, the lead platoon, of 'A' Company wrote:

> "....an intense bombardment was in progress on our front line and support trenches by the time I took my platoon out. Cannister bombs, high explosives and shrapnel catching all men as they reached the support line. This curtain of fire was extended to our support trenches. The heavy guns appeared to be working from Puisieux and the shrapnel from Serre. My platoon was in Dunmow and my line of advance about 20 yards south of SAP A.

> Our artillery seemed to me to have been concentrating mainly on the German trenches with good effect in smashing them up, but evidently, judging by the rifle fire, it did not smash up their dug-outs."

In his report Captain A. D. Stephenson, who commanded 'C' Company wrote:

> "...the enemy artillery was a great surprise to our troops who had expected to find most of the enemy guns put out of action. The enemy infantry, standing on the parapet firing at our advancing troops, seemed to consider themselves quite

safe from our guns. Could our advancing troops not have laid down while our guns shelled the enemy down with shrapnel?'

Captain Stephenson went on to point out that, although the platoons moved off in four lines, the lack of bridges over the trenches to be crossed, and the width of these trenches due to the shelling, had caused the lines of men to 'bunch' at each crossing, a point that did not go unnoticed by the German machine gunners. He also suggested that, had the brigade machine gun teams been given a more flexible role, they could have been used to enfilade the enemy parapet, or to combat his machine guns. 'C' Company were the last to leave the assembly trenches and all four platoons reached the British front line. Few, however, were able to advance beyond it. Nevertheless, it was reported that Lieutenant Akam, of 'B' Company reached the German front line with his platoon as did Sergeant Bullock, the Battalion's Signals Sergeant, together with one man and a party of men from the 4th Division.

Corporal Goldthorpe had scrambled out behind Lieutenant Foizey with his section of 'Bombers', each wearing a canvas waistcoat with pockets for eight Mills grenades in addition to carrying a rifle and bayonet. Their task, on reaching the objective, was to proceed another 150 yards down a communication trench and build a barricade to forestall any counter attack. Having travelled not more than 30 yards or so the section was reduced to four men. Lieutenant Foizey ordered his small party to take cover behind a small hillock, whilst he went forward to see what was happening; but he was killed after covering only a couple of yards. Now there was not a living soul in sight. It was obvious that they could not go forward, but they had been warned that anyone who returned to the trenches unwounded would be shot.

After some considerable time, when things appeared to have quietened down a little, a Private Smith volunteered to bo back for instructions. Although he was continually fired on he managed to do so, and returned to within hailing distance with instructions to go back. Corporal Goldthorpe ordered the remaining two to go back in short dashes at three minute intervals, following himself three minutes after the last man.

Despite heavy fire all safely reached their own lines. Here they joined about twenty other men and the only surviving officer in "A" Company.

Private Frank Hartley had reached and crossed the front line trenches from which the 15th Battalion had started. He went on. The earth all around him was being thrown up in a spray by exploding shells, whilst the sky rained clods of earth. Suddenly, he felt a heavy blow and his right leg crumpled under him, pouring blood. Around him bursting shrapnel shells were turning wounded into dead so he crawled back half a mile, dragging Ralph Holmeswith him, until he found ground offering some shelter from the barrage. Then he fell unconscious.

By 9.00 a.m. the front line trenches were crowded with men but with no officers or N.C.O.'s to organize them. Let us take up Sergeant Major Cussons' story again.

'. . . I made my way to what I took to be Brigade Headquarters, as I saw a board to that effect, but it turned out to be the 94th Brigade. They telephoned my information to Division and also gave me orders to proceed to 93rd Brigade Headquarters. This took some time and on getting to Sackville Street, I was ordered, with others, to line that trench in the need to quell a German counter attack which had just started (this report proved to be false). As soon as the necessity for this was over, I reported myself to the 93rd Brigade Headquarters who told me that what was left of the 16th Battalion were being collected in Sackville Street and that I was to return there and look after them.

In the day, somewhere between 3.00 and 4.00 p.m. in the afternoon, I was ordered to form up the remainder of the battalion in Legend Street, near Brigade Headquarters. After two hours I was ordered to take the battalion down to Dunmow trench, which I did.

During the wait at Brigade Headquarters, I took the names and numbers of the men of the Regiment who I had with me, about fifty in all. Just as I was going down to Dunmow trench, the first reinforcements, in the form of Officers and N.C.O.'s arrived. Until the arrival of these reinforcements, I had no N.C.O. with me above the rank of Lance Corporal."

In point of fact Lieutenant Ransome was sent to Monk trench at 9.00 a.m. to try to reorganize the battalion. He was killed very shortly afterwards.

At 9.50 a.m. the Brigadier General left his Headquarters for the front line to make a personal assessment of the situation. By 11.45 a.m. he had returned and decided that any further attempt to advance would be fruitless due to the heavy casualties that had been suffered and also that there were scarcely any officers or N.C.O.'s available.

Lt. Colonel H. F. G. Carter

In front of the British trenches, the dead and wounded lay in clumps whilst the German parapet was manned by confident troops who sniped at anything which moved. Here and there a wounded man, still able to lift a rifle, sniped back.

The front line was now held by Lieutenant Peace, who was wounded and looking very ill, Lieutenant Whitaker and Lieutenant Cross, all of the 18th Battalion, and about 200 men of all Regiments. The Durhams had two companies in Monk trench and one company in Maitland trench. Fearing a counter attack, Brigade now ordered the Durhams to hold the front line where possible, although much of it was now untenable, with a company in support in Monk trench. What was left of the 16th Battalion was withdrawn to Dunmow trench which they were ordered to hold. Major H. H. Kennedy was given command of the Battalion.

At 4.00 p.m., on instructions from Divisional Headquarters, Major H. F. G. Carter reported to Brigade Headquarters and assumed command of the 18th Battalion whose survivors were then being collected by Lieutenant-Colonel Bowes of the 18th Durhams. At that time there were some sixty members of the Battalion in Dunmow trench. Major Carter searched Grey,

Advanced Dressing Station, Somme, 1916. *Imperial War Museum, Negative Q2023.*

Bradford, Monk and Bleneau trenches and 'SAP A' for survivors but, apart from a few wounded, found these trenches deserted. At 8.45 p.m. he received orders to occupy and hold Monk trench. By then he had with him Lieutenants Cross and Howarth, 2nd Lieutenants Whitaker, Stephenson and Thornton and 120 other ranks. Later, he received orders to retire to Languard trench after being relieved by the 92nd Brigade who were to attack Serre on the following day. The plan for this attack was subsequently abandoned.

On the right, during the afternoon, another Bradford battalion, the 6th (Territorial) Battalion of the Regiment, had fallen in heaps in their attack on Theipval.

During the night of July 1st/2nd stretcher bearers of the 11th Battalion East Yorkshire Regiment together with rations and reinforcements of 75 men per battalion arrived in the line. The Brigade War Diary for the 2nd and 3rd read respectively "quiet day in front - wounded and dead brought in" and "nothing to report, wounded and dead brought in all day". As soon as night fell parties were formed as stretcher bearers to bring in wounded still lying out in the open, and to identify the dead who were too numerous to bring in. Those who performed this task were never to forget it. As they turned over bodies so as to retrieve pay books from breast pockets and red identification discs from around the neck (green discs to be left to enable a later identification of the bodies), the violent manner of their deaths was revealed. Here were men with only half a face, with an empty brain cavity, or chest or stomach cavity. Here men with no limbs, even heads. The ground they walked on was carpeted with intestines, bits of men and offal.

Here and there wounded men called out for help, some babbled in delirium whilst others breathed with that horrible gurgling, snorting snore of those who are seriously hurt. Great numbers lay still, breathing shallowly. Many of these were left for dead.

There seems to have been an unwritten truce as this work went on long after daybreak, the Germans, presumably, were also carrying their wounded out of the trenches.

Later, men were brought in who had lain, badly wounded, in shell holes for up to two days. Amongst these was one of the few surviving officers from the 15th Battalion. There was Dick Collins, who had lain unconscious for two days with half his face torn away, having been left for dead. Fortunately, he had regained consciousness in time, and was able to attract attention. In contrast, Frank Hartley woke up to find himself in a field hospital with a red tag pinned to his blanket, indicating that his wounded leg was to be amputated. Fortunately for Frank, the arrival of another train-load of wounded diverted attention, and his wounded leg was left to heal of its own accord.

After dark the Germans left their trenches and searched in front of the wire for survivors. In his book *A Victorian Son* Stuart Cloete, whose battalion months later recovered British dead from the proximity of the then abandoned German front line, said that the wounded had been despatched by bayonetting them in the throat, whilst the skulls of the dead were smashed as if by sledge hammer. He said of these dead: They hung like washing on the barbs [of the wire], like scarecrows who scared no crows since they were edible."

At noon on the 4th of July a severe thunderstorm caused heavy flooding of the trenches, in some cases up to four feet deep, which created great difficulties in evacuating the wounded who were now laying in heaps around the Casualty Clearing Station in Basin Wood. Here Major MacTavish and Captains Roche and Horner worked in shirt sleeves, non stop, at trestle tables with the dead piled around them. Captain E. V. Tempest of the Regiment's 6th Battalion, describing a Casualty Clearing Station further to the South, *Paisley Dump*, wrote:

> ". . . as one approached, one became aware of a noise a noise inhuman. A wail as of enormous fingers on an enormous wet glass, a wail that rose and fell, interminable, unbearable. Then suddenly one became aware whence the wail came. All along the muddy roadway they lay - the wounded, hundreds of them, brown blanket shapes, some muttering, some moaning, some singing in delirium, some quite still."

Major MacTavish, a Canadian serving with the 18th Battalion, was to write to a friend: "I'll never forget July 1st as long as I live. It was an awful day."

On July 1st,. at 10.00 a.m., Fred Rawnsley wrote in his diary: "Rumours that advance has been successful". At 12.00 a.m. he added: "Wounded commenced to struggle through. Heartrending sight. Pals badly smashed up. Thank God I didn't take part."

On the evening of July 1st, before going to dinner, Field-Marshal Haig wrote in his diary "I am inclined to believe from further reports that few of VIII Corps left their trenches".

George Morgan spent the 2nd and 3rd of July helping to carry stretcher cases from Basin Wood to Euston Dump, the collecting point for ambulances. Here he found Billy Booth laying on a stretcher. He had lain in the open for three days waiting to be collected as had Corporal Metcalf. Billy Booth died of his wounds. Corporal Metcalf survived but was to walk with a limp for the rest of his life. He helped to carry out Abe Waddington, the Yorkshire Cricketer, who grumbled loudly at every bump or jolt. When finally they arrived at Euston Dump a Medical Officer read Private Waddington's wound tag and ordered him to "get off the stretcher and walk to the ambulance". After some remonstrations, Private Waddington did as he was ordered! Later George Morgan was called down to Bus-les-Artois where he found his friend, Bill Kenny, laying on a table, paralysed from the neck down. He said "Will you write to my fiancee, George, and tell her I shall soon be with her?" The medical orderly slowly shook his head. Bill Kenny died shortly afterwards. George kept his promise.

On the evening of July 4th, the Brigade was relieved by the 144th Infantry Brigade. The journey out of the trenches occupied a great deal of time, hampered by the flooded condition of the trenches caused by torrential rain, and by the numerous stretcher cases which still clogged many of the bays. Further difficulties arose when the 94th Brigade accidentally used Railway Avenue instead of Northern Avenue. As they struggled along Northern Avenue a voice from the dark called out: "Come on, boys, only another dozen yards." A rather short soldier, who hailed from Halifax, replied in a loud, clear voice: "It's awreet for thee thi big bugger, arz almust drowning down 'ere!" This brought a titter back from the darkness. Apparently his remark was addressed to the Divisional Commander.

The remnants of the 16th Battalion were led out by a Lieutenant of the Royal Engineers in whose charge they had been placed. This gentleman was newly commissioned from the ranks and wore a private soldier's uniform with cloth pips sewn on his shoulder straps. His small stature earned him the nickname 'four-by-two' after the piece of cloth used to clean the bore of rifles. While his simple attire caused George and his friends some amusement he was, unlike many of his brother officers, at least dressed in accordance with orders (see page 28). He later accused George Morgan of losing his 'British Warmer' which, he said, he had placed in his charge. From subsequent enquiries it was learnt that the missing coat had been placed on the back of a limber by another private. The limber had then been driven off at full gallop before the unfortunate private could retrieve it.

Both battalions then moved to Louvencourt on the same day, the 16th via Colin Camps where they ate a meal and were greeted by the villagers with a glass of wine. The 18th moved via Bertrancourt where there was a welcome issue of tea and rum. They were told that there would be no Reveille - *they could sleep as long as they wished.*

However, on the 5th of July after only four hours sleep, both battalions were paraded and addressed by the Corps Commander, Lieutenant-General Hunter-Weston, mounted on his charger and flanked by two Lancers. His address is reproduced here:

FROM: Lieut-Gen. Sir Aylmer Hunter-Weston, K.C.B., D.S.O.

TO: All officers, N.C.O.'s and men of the VIII Army Corps

"In so big a command as an Army Corps of four Divisions (about 80,000 men) it is impossible for me to come round all front line trenches and all billets to see every man as I wish to do. You must take the will for the deed, and accept this printed message in place of the spoken word.

It is difficult for me to express my admiration for the splendid courage, determination and discipline displayed by every Officer, N.C.O. and man of the battalions that took part in the great attack on the Beaumont-Hamel-Serre position on the 1st July. All observers agree in stating that the various waves of men issued from their trenches and moved forward at the appointed time in perfect order, undismayed by the heavy artillery fire and deadly machine gun fire. There were no cowards nor waverers, and not a man fell out. It was a magnificent display of disciplined courage worthy of the best traditions of the British race.

Very few are left of my old comrades, the original 'Contemptibles' but their successors in the 4th Division have shown that they are worthy to bear the honours gained by the 4th Division at their first great fight at Fontaine-au-Pire and Ligny, during the great Retreat and greater Advance across the Marne and Aisne, and in all the hard fighting at Ploegsteert and at Ypres.

Though but few of my old comrades, the heroes of the historic landing at Cape Helles, are still with us, the 29th Division of today has shown itself capable of maintaining its high traditions, and has proved itself worthy of its hard earned title of 'The Incomparable 29th'.

The 31st New Army Division and the 48th Territorial Division, by the heroism and discipline of the units, engaged in this, their first big battle, have proved themselves worthy to fight by the side of such magnificent regular Divisions as the 4th and 29th. There can be no higher praise.

We had the most difficult part of the line to attack. The Germans had fortified it with skill and immense labour for many months, they had kept their best troops here, and had assembled north, east and south-east of it a formidable collection of artillery and many machine guns.

By your splendid attack you held these enemy forces here in the north and so enabled our friends in the south, both British and French, to achieve the brilliant success that they have. Therefore, though we did not do all we hoped to do, you have more than pulled your weight, and you and our even more glorious comrades who have preceded us across the Great Divide have nobly done your duty.

We have got to stick it out and go on hammering. Next time we attack, if it please God, we will not only pull our weight but will pull off a big thing. With such troops as you, who are determined to stick it out and do your duty, we are certain of winning through to a glorious victory.

I salute each Officer, N.C.O. and Man of the 4th, 29th, 31st and 48th Divisions as a comrade-in-arms and I rejoice to have the privilege of commanding such a band of heroes as the VIII Corps have proved themselves to be."

H. Q., VIII Corps	AYLMER HUNTER_WESTON
4th July, 1916	Lieutenant-General

Lieutenant-Colonel Carter said that the three battalions of the West Yorkshire Regiment, and the Company of the Durhams, advanced into the enemy fire, rifles held at the port "as if on parade."

The 16th Battalion went into the line with a strength of 24 officers, including medical officers, and 750 other ranks. During the period June 30th to July 3rd, they lost 11 officers killed, one missing and ten wounded. 69 other ranks killed or died of wounds, 111 missing and 313 wounded, a total of 515, or nearly 67% of the strength. The 18th Battalion's casualties were 16 officers and 400 other ranks, only seven officers and 170 other ranks surviving, a loss of 70%.

Lieutenant-Colonel Maurice Nicholl Kennard was born in 1883, the second son of Mr and Mrs Robert William Kennard. In

1903 he joined the 6th Dragoon Guards from the Militia, and, after holding the adjutancy of the Regiment for a period from April 1910 he became Captain in 1913. Whilst serving with the Dragoon Guards in the early days of the war he was wounded and was mentioned in dispatches as early as October 1914. In 1915 he was promoted to Major and took command of the 13th Battalion of the York and Lancaster Regiment, later to be transferred to the command of the 18th Battalion of the West Yorkshire Regiment. His body was never found; his name appears on the Thiepval Memorial as 'Missing with no known grave.'

Captain Pringle, the commander of 'C' Company of whom Lieutenant Laxton had spoken, was killed. His body was found 20 years later and interred in Sucrerie Cemetery, near Colin Camps.

The body of 2nd Lieutenant Simms was never found, nor was that of his Company Commander, Captain Donald C. Smith, despite the efforts of his father Mr. E. J. Smith, a Bradford councillor. Before the war, Donald Smith had played rugby for Yorkshire and, despite his spartan ways, which were the cause of some amusement amongst those he led, he was regarded by all as a very brave officer.

Lieutenant Robert Sutcliffe, a distinguished looking man in his mid-thirties, died of wounds whilst travelling back to England on a hospital ship. An old boy of Bradford Grammar School, he joined the public school's battalion of the Middlesex Regiment at the outbreak of war and later obtained a commission in his County Regiment. He is buried in Yorkshire, near his family home at Slackhouse.

The body of Private Dawson Horne, who "couldn't wait to get at 'em", was recovered from the German wire on August 8th, 1916. Unfortunately the location of his grave was lost and his name is to be found on the Memorial for the Missing on Thiepal Ridge. The body of Lieutenant Harold Egbert Foizey, is buried in Euston Road Cemetery, on the site then known as Euston Dump.

Among the missing was Private Harry Redman, of just twenty years. In an age when those bereaved, especially by dramatic tragedy, receive help and counselling, it is difficult to imagine the feelings of Harry Redman's parents who received only a telegram bearing the bald statement that their son was *missing in action.* Until the day of her death Mrs Redman never accepted that her son was dead, insisting that he was alive in some hospital having lost his memory.

Private Harry Redman

Also listed amongst the dead was Private William Whitaker, aged 17 years and 10 months.

Sir Douglas Haig's Staff Officer was to write 'It would seem as if the only differences that numbers in an attack make to a properly located machine gun defence, when there is light and time to see, is to provide a better target'. With regard to this piece of wisdom Sir Winston Churchill was to comment: "No one can quarrel with such a conclusion.'

Frank Burn (centre) with Fred Hall and Frank Booth standing in the remains of the British Front Line facing Serre, July 1st., 1966. *Bradford Telegraph and Argus.*

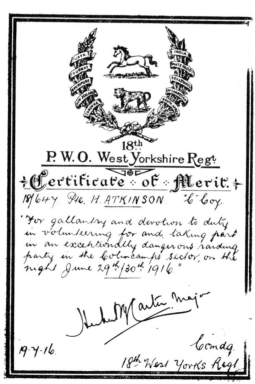

Private H. Atkinson's Certificate of Merit for gallantry on the night before.

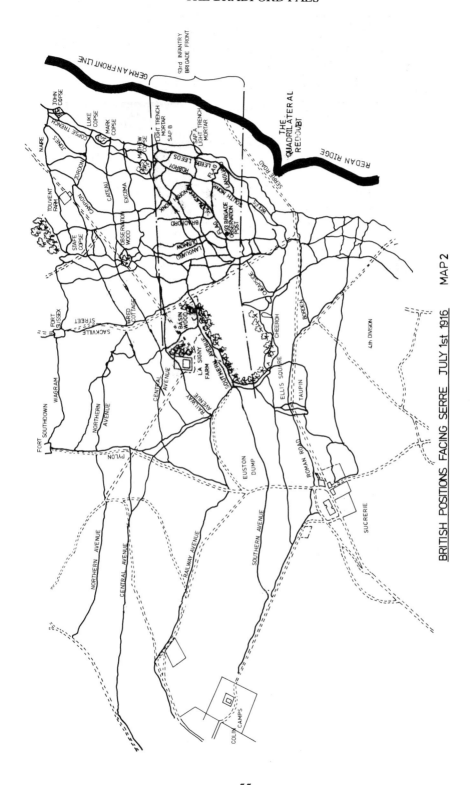

BRITISH POSITIONS FACING SERRE JULY 1st 1916   MAP 2

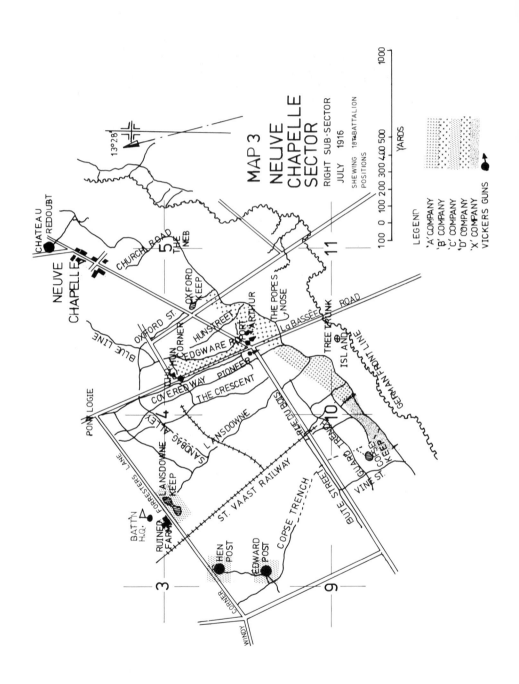

Shrapnel balls picked up by the author from the fields of the Somme with a pound coin for comparison.

CHAPTER 4: NEUVE CHAPELLE, FESTUBERT, GIVENCHY

Through darkness curves a spume of falling flares
That flood the field with shallow, blanching light.
The huddled sentry stares . . . .
Siegfried Sassoon

On July 6th, both battalions left the Somme area. The 16th Battalion marched to Lestram, where they spent almost three weeks before moving to Les Lobes. The 18th Battalion marched to L'Ecleme. Here they were addressed by the Divisional Commander who congratulated them on the fighting of July 1st to the 4th and spoke of the necessity to inspire all reinforcements with the same efficient spirit as that shown by all ranks. He expressed his extreme regret that the Battalion had lost so many officers, N.C.O.'s and men, especially their Commanding Officer, Lieutenant-Colonel Kennard.

On July 27th, the 18th Battalion plus a composite company from the 16th, known as 'X' Company, took over the front line trenches from the 13th York and Lancaster Regiment in the Neuve Chapelle Right Sub Sector. Here, unlike the valley of the Somme, the landscape was flat and enclosed. Owing to the wet nature of the ground the defences consisted, in the main, of breast works. The front line had, before the Battle of Neuve Chapelle, been the German third and fourth support lines. Most men who fought in this sector were never to forget the dead, most of them British, who lay in putrescent rows in No-man's-land. It was said that parapets were built up with them and that corpses served as land-marks for patrols and direction aids to dug-outs and communication trenches. In his history of the 6th (Territorial) Battalion of the Regiment. Captain E. V. Tempest described the area as "a vast cemetery where no one had been buried" and said that "the heavy stench which lay like a cloud over the trenches, could be felt miles away."

On completion of the relief, Headquarters Company had established themselves in the ruined farm in Square S3d. 'X' Company held the right section. 'A' Company, commanded by Lieutenant R S. Cross, held the centre section and 'B' Company, led by Lieutenant L. C. Watson, held the left section of the sub-sector. 'D' Company, commanded by Lieutenant A. Howarth, were in support at Port Arthur and Edgware Road, Captain B. Tooke, together with 2nd Lieutenant J. L. Wood and 'C' Company, were in reserve at Lansdown Post, Hen Post and Edward Post. These positions are shown in Map 3.

In the meantime the 16th Battalion, less the composite company, marched to Croix Barbes and took over from the 11th East Lancashire Regiment the front line posts, 'Rags,' 'Bones,' 'Grotto,' 'Angle' and Saint Vaast, Loretto and Euston. The verdict of the Field General Courts Martial (dated 14th July, 1916) who had considered Private Patchet's crime of 'writing by candlelight' was now received and he departed to base to begin his sentence - after his experience on July 1st, perhaps thankfully. Nevertheless, by todays standards this would seem a strange reward for a gallant soldier.

At 9.30 p.m. on the night of the 27th, the 18th Battalion left company section, came under heavy H.E., shrapnel and *minen werfer* bombardment, whilst the entire front line was swept continuously by machine gun fire. At 10.27 p.m., a runner from 'D' Company arrived at Battalion Headquarters saying that German troops had broken into the front line trenches 10 minutes previously, and Lieutenant Howarth had sent a message to Port Arthur for bombers, as he had none with him. Brigade ordered 'D' Company to launch an immediate counter-attack.

At 11.30 p.m. Private H. L. Riley of 'B' Company arrived at Battalion Headquarters supporting Corporal Lee who was wounded. He said that a *minen werfer* had struck a sentry post and immediately afterwards a party of Germans, dressed in black, 25 to 30 strong, had broken into the trench. The Germans, in two parties of about 16, armed with pistols and bombs and under one officer, broke into the British front line at two points: working inwards. On uniting they left with several prisoners, including Dickie Bond. Their arrival was unexpected and rapid, they advanced under cover of their own bombardment and broke into the line immediately after the barrage lifted. Many of the *Pals* were surprised in their dug-outs, the first inkling of the raid being when electric torches carried by the raiders flashed in their faces. Corporal Lee and Private Riley were in such a dug-out when a German, armed with a pistol and a Knob Kerry or, perhaps, a hand grenade, threw a light on them and told them to put up their hands. Lee and Riley made a dash for it and got away; Lee being hit in the leg whilst making his escape.

When they left, the trench was held by Germans. Those who were not taken prisoner defended themselves with rifles but were reluctant to use bombs for fear of injuring their comrades. Witnesses reported that several of the enemy inflicted slight wounds on their prisoners, presumably to prevent them escaping, although it is noteworthy that one man was bandaged up by a German who had wounded him first with a bomb and then a pistol. Lance Corporal Denton of 'B' Company was taken prisoner in this trench and led about 300 yards towards the German line. There he knocked over his man and escaped, reaching his own lines at about 10.00 a.m. the following morning. He was slightly wounded. Lieutenants Howarth and Watson and 2nd Lieutenant Walton were all taken prisoner. According to a soldier who was left behind because of his wounds, the raiders were in the front line for about twenty minutes. In addition to their prisoners they took away with them a Vickers gun and a box of ammunition. A dead German left in the trench was identified as a member of the 3rd Ersatz Company of the 248th Ersatz Battalion Reserve Infantry Regiment. This identification was made from the only document found on his body, his leave pass from April, 1916.

Captain Harry H. Dalley

When news of the raid was received at Battalion Headquarters, 'B' and 'D' Companies were ordered to report their situation. In the meantime a message was received from Brigade that 150 men of the 15th Battalion were proceeding down Lansdown. 'C' Company was ordered to move to reinforce 'D' Company by way of 'Covered way' as soon as the 15th Battalion men arrived. Runners brought in news that 'B' Company was uncertain of the situation but that they had a bombing party proceeding to clear the line from the left. At 12.50 a.m. a message, timed 11.35 p.m. was received from the officer then commanding 'D' Company, probably the Adjutant, Captain Harry L. Dalley, which read: "Am in front line of 'B' Company. Have found Williams but practically only ten 'B' Company men. Am manning front line with 25 men. Several wounded but cannot spare men to bring them out. No bosche. Lieutenants Burton and Fletcher with me".

By 4.00 a.m. the front line had been reinforced and a party of sappers despatched to repair the heavy damage in the trenches caused by the shell fire. In the preceding affairs the Battalion had lost six killed, including Lieutenant Cross, 2nd Lieutenant W. R. Humphries and Company Sergeant Major G. H. Lipton, 42 wounded, of whom four died later, and 36 missing, believed prisoners.

From this time, until the Battalion was relieved on August 4th, little of significance beyond patrol activity, enemy sniping and shelling, is recorded in the War Diary. On that day the 16th Battalion was relieved by the 13th Battalion the York and Lancaster Regiment and marched to billets in Les Lobes whilst the 18th Battalion were relieved by a composite battalion of the

16th East Yorkshire Regiment and the 11th and 12th York and Lancaster Regiment, and moved to billets in Lestram. The composite company, X Company, rejoined their own battalion after their spell of duty with the 18th but less Sergeant W. Culling of 'D' Company and Lance Corporal McConnel and Privates J. Moore, Cussons and W. Ackroyd, all of 'C' Company who had lost their lives in the preceding actions.

After a few days rest in billets, both battalions received orders to take over the Festubert left sub-sector. Both had completed the relief by midnight on August 10th, the 16th Battalion occupying positions on the right, the 18th Battalion on the left. The terrain was similar to the Neuve Chapelle sector, the defences consisting, in the main, of breast works. This was a sector in which enemy snipers were constantly active and in which the parapet was swept at regular intervals by machine gun fire. Enemy artillery was very active, making Cover, Richmond, Shetland and Pioneer trenches particularly unhealthy locations. On the evening of the 15th, the 18th Battalion suffered four casualties, one other rank killed and three wounded by snipers. One sniper was reported to be in Canadian Orchard, not 60 yards from their positions.

A patrol which attempted to move into No-man's-land from three successive bays was met by sniper fire on each occasion. On the following evening snipers again prevented a patrol from going out from Islands 31 and 32 and also drove back a wiring party.

On the night of the 17th, the 18th Battalion were relieved by the 11th East Yorkshire Regiment and moved to billets in Rue de L'Epinette as mobile reserve. 'B' Company and 30 men from 'A' Company however, remained in the trenches moving to the right sub-sector in the old British front line and coming under the orders of the 15th West Yorkshire Regiment. The following day the 16th Battalion was relieved by the 11th East Yorkshire Regiment. Four officers and 75 other ranks were attached to the 15th Battalion of the Regiment whilst the remainder of the Battalion took over the defence of the Village Line which consisted of five posts named Le Plantin North, Festubert (Central), Festubert (East), Cailloux South, Cailloux East and various other small posts. Shortly after occupying these

31st Division Men in a SAP-Head, Givenchy. *Imperial War Museum, Q7265.*

positions Lieutenant A. S. Gibson suffered a serious wound to the left hand and was evacuated to a casualty clearing station and, subsequently, struck off the strength.

The Givenchy sector had been very active, the Engineers on both sides competing to blow up large mines beneath opposing trenches. The sector became a line of very large craters with both sides building saps on their sides of the craters. Being only yards from each other there was considerable hand and rifle grenade activity from both sides. At 8 pm. on the 20th, a mine was blown by the enemy in the Givenchy Sector which destroyed 'I SAP'. This was followed by a heavy bombardment which switched on to the right of the Festubert section, being particularly intense between Islands 9 and 13. At 8.45 p.m. the barrage lifted on to the old British lines and then dropped again on to the front line. At this time a strong party of the enemy attempted to force an entry into the British lines between Islands 10a, 11 and 12, but were driven off without achieving their objective. A barrage was put down in No-man's-land in an attempt to cut off their retreat. Later a patrol went out to try to obtain identification, but failed to find any dead or wounded.

The 16th Battalion received news in August that Major H H. Kennedy was promoted to the rank of Acting Lieutenant-Colonel. Sergeant A. W. Ashforth was granted a field commission, becoming a 2nd Lieutenant with the Battalion. Also, Company Sergeant Major G. Cussons and Private T.Pearson were both awarded the Distinguished Conduct Medal for bravery in action and for their devotion to duty on July 1st, 1916.

The first part of September found the 16th Battalion in the right sub-section in the Neuve Chapelle section of trenches. The 18th Battalion were located in the Festubert left sub-section occupying positions in Hun Street and Port Arthur.

The 18th Battalion then spent a few days resting at Croix Barbes, but mid-September found both battalions employed in the right sub-sector of the Givenchy sector. As the month closed, the 16th Battalion were holding the 'Village Line', a series of posts known as 'Givenchy Keep', 'Orchard Redoubt', 'Moat Farm', 'Hilders Redoubt', 'Herts Redoubt', and 'Pont Fixe South'. The 18th Battalion were occupying positions at 'Windy Corner' and in 'Poppy Redoubt'.

On October 3rd, the 31st Division was taken out of the line and moved to the Bethune area. After a brief respite in billets in the town the 18th Battalion moved to billets in L'Ecleme whilst the 16th marched to La Miquellerie. Here they occupied billets which had been organized by 2nd Lieutenant E. Wilson, the billeting officer, and Sergeant Harry Drake, the Battalion interpreter. Harry Drake in later years was to teach in several Bradford schools and was to be revered by generations of young Bradfordians.

On the 7th October, the 93rd Infantry Brigade, left the 1st Army area, marching to Lillers where they entrained for Doullens, arriving in the late afternoon. Here they detrained and marched to the village of Thievres where the 18th Battalion took billets. The 16th marched on to billets in Famechon.

In October news was received that Captain Harry L. Dalley, Adjutant of the 18th Battalion, had been awarded the Military Cross for his conspicuous gallantry during the recent fighting and that Major H. F. G. Carter was promoted to the rank of Lieutenant Colonel.

Captain Harry Dalley with his wife after receiving the Military Cross at Buckingham Palace from George V on June 20th, 1917.

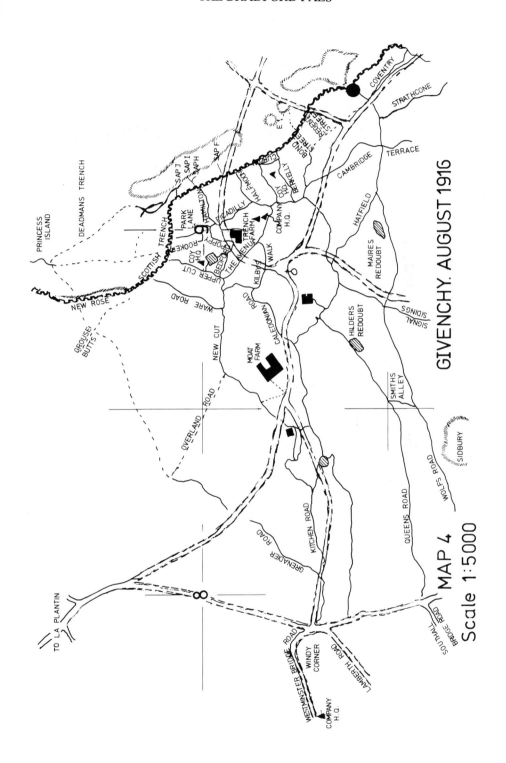

GIVENCHY. AUGUST 1916

MAP 4

Scale 1:5000

No-man's land in front of Serre, 1916. Imperial War Museum, *Neg. Q1910*

CHAPTER 5: HEBUTERNE

I see them in foul dug-outs, gnawed by rats,
And in the ruined trenches, lashed with rain,
Dreaming of things they did with balls and bats,
And mocked by hopeless longing to regain
Bank holidays, and picture shows, and spats,
And going to the office in the train.
Siegfried Sassoon.

On October 21st, the 93rd Brigade took over the Hebuterne
Sector, the 16th Battalion occupying the right sub-section with
the 18th Battalion on the left (see map 5). This sector had
originally been held by the French, who had made several novel
innovations. In the centre of the village they had sunk a deep
well into which drained several others. It was equipped with a
pump, driven by a petrol engine, so that there was always a
plentiful supply of water. Under a small waterfall they had
installed a turbine-driven generator which supplied electricity to
light the numerous deep dug-outs in the village. A number of
communication trenches radiated from the village, three of the
most important being Yellow Street, Yankee Street and Woman
Street. The latter got its name from the decomposing body of a
young woman which had been discovered near its entrance in a
pool of putrid water, once the village pond.

Here undulating country, long grass and bushes, provided excellent opportunities for patrol activity, particularly 'Winkling', an activity first practised by the Canadians. This exercise involved a small party surprising an enemy sentry in an isolated post and then winkling prisoners out of the dug-outs behind him.

On the night of the 23rd and again on the night of the 26th, the 16th Battalion sent out a raiding party under 2nd Lieutenants C. P. Graham and D. T. King with 30 other ranks. Their intention was to find two gaps in the enemy wire, previously reconnoitred, and to penetrate the German line. On both these occasions they were unsuccessful, finding the gaps to have been filled.

On the night of the 24th, 2nd Lieutenant D. A. Gill, Sergeant G. Quigley and Private H. Sutcliffe of the 18th Battalion left their lines at 8.45 p.m. to investigate the German wire. They proceeded eastward to the enemy wire and then about 100 yards to the south, where they found a gap, about 30 yards wide. They proceeded through the gap to within 10 yards of the enemy parapet. Unfortunately at this point they were seen by a German sentry who fired three shots, mortally wounding 2nd Lieutenant Gill. The enemy immediately swept the area with machine gun fire. Sergeant Quigley and Private Sutcliffe succeeded in extricating themselves from their predicament and returned to their own lines, unwounded and carrying their officer's body.

Both battalions were relieved from the front line on October 26th, and returned to support billets in Sailly aux Bois. From there they provided nightly working parties and fighting patrols.

Again on the night of the 27th a raiding party of 30 other ranks led by 2nd Lieutenants J. Luke and H. R. Mason, left the lines at 10.30 p.m., intent on penetrating the enemy trenches. Unfortunately whilst the advanced parties were engaged in getting through the wire nearest the enemy trenches they were spotted by a sentry and heavily fired on. They were compelled to withdraw, suffering one other rank killed. 2nd Lieutenant Luke and three other ranks were wounded.

On the 30th October the 16th proceeded to billets in Thievres whilst 'C' and 'D' Companies of the 18th went into bivouacs near Courcelles. The rest of the Battalion went into hutments at Coigneux. Both battalions now enjoyed a brief respite from front line duties but, on November 7th, they moved back into support billets in Sailly aux Bois. On the 11th November, between the hours of 10.00 p.m. and 3.00 a.m. and again at 6.00 a.m. the village was heavily shelled with high explosives and gas shells.

One of the last H. E. shells fired in this bombardment was a direct hit on one of the 16th Battalion's billets, killing eight other ranks and wounding 11 others, including 2nd Lieutenant G. Nicholls.

November 13th marked the beginning of the British offensive on both banks of the River Ancre. The 18th Battalion occupied the Hebuterne left sub-sector whilst 'A' and 'C' Companies of the 16th Battalion occupied the left company section of the right sub-sector, coming under the command of the 18th. 'B' and 'D' Companies remained in bivouacs at Sailly aux Bois under the command of Major G. S. Blagbrough pending further orders. Lieutenant-Colonel Kennedy moved his headquarters into the dug-out which housed the 18th. Headquarters in Vercingetorix trench. The battalions were to hold the line during the attack on Serre and the German positions further south, while two battalions of the 92nd Brigade attacked on their front to cover the left flank of the assault. Zero hour was fixed at 5.45 a.m. when the British barrage opened promptly. Until 7.45 a.m. the enemy made no attempt to fire upon the front trenches. From then until 10.00 a.m. the enemy exhibited slightly more activity, shelling Brissoux and Knox trenches. This shelling became less as the morning advanced until about 11.45 a.m. when a heavy barrage was opened, chiefly directed at Jena Bart and Knox trenches and the junction of Jena and Vercingetorix trenches. During this time the 16th suffered ten casualties. The 18th Battalion suffered similarly. Just before noon 'C' Company Signals dug-out was blown in, killing two and wounding three. By 12.30 p.m. 'C' Company had lost nine dead and ten wounded. The bombardment slackened shortly after noon but increased to an intense barrage again around 2 pm., costing the 16th a further ten casualties. The barrage had slackened by early evening, leaving the two battalions with a total of 55 casualtie suffered.

The tour continued with spells in the trenches and brief respites in billets at Rossignol farm or Sailly aux Bois, although these 'respites' included the provision of working and carrying parties to, and into, the front line. On December 3rd, whilst occupying the right sub-sector the 16th Battalion were subjected to a heavy *minenwerfer* bombardment. The enemy scored one hit which killed five and wounded three other ranks.

Some relief from the monotony and hardships of trench life was provided to the 18th Battalion on December 9th when, around noon, an enemy deserter was seen approaching their lines along the Gommecourt-Hebuterne road. He was taken into custody and found to be very drunk. The inebriated German soldier was escorted to Brigade Headquarters.

On the same day the 16th received news that Corporal C. Higgins had been awarded the Distinguished Conduct Medal for gallantry and devotion to duty.

On December 23rd, Major G. S. Blagbrough was killed during a whizz-bang bombardment of the 16th Battalion's front. The Major, a former master at Bridlington Grammar School where he had been known affectionately by his pupils as *Blags*, had been with the Battalion since its formation and was second-in-command at the time of his death.

On December 31st, the 93rd Infantry Brigade were relieved by the 92nd Infantry Brigade. The 16th moved to Coigneux to rest but the 18th Battalion were required to remain in Hebuterne Keep and Sailly aux Bois until January 10th, 1917, when they were relieved in the front line by the 8th Battalion of the Gloucester Regiment.

The entire Brigade then spent over a month resting in the Doullens-Bernaville area. During this period both battalions commenced training in accordance with the newly introduced system of platoon organization under which platoon and company officers were entirely responsible for the training of their units including bombers, Lewis gunners and rifle grenadiers. Work was principally devoted to platoon drill, musketry, reorganization of platoons and route marching. Only half each working day was devoted to these tasks, the remainder on alternate afternoons and mornings by half battalions, being set aside for recreation. Football matches, running, tug-of-war, bayonet fighting, bomb throwing, and boxing matches were organized and all men, the diaries record, took part.

In January, Lieutenant-Colonel Kennedy left the Battalion to command the 6th Battalion of his own Regiment, the Scottish Rifles. A tall genteel Scot, he always insisted on wearing the 'trews' and glengarry of his own Regiment, and was well liked and respected by all. His place was taken by Lieutenant-Colonel A. C. Croydon, an officer who had risen from the ranks. Before receiving his commission he had been a Sergeant Major in the Lincolnshire Regiment. He was a strict disciplinarian of gruff manner. Coming events were to prove him a very proficient and professional officer.

Public concern at this time caused the War Office to forbid the employment of soldiers under the age of nineteen in the front line. Lance-Corporal Morgan and nineteen other young soldiers were, therefore, detached for instructional duties at the Infantry Training Depot at Etaples, known to British Tommies as *Eat Apples*. The Depot included a large tract of land laid out with trenches, barbed wire, etc., known to soldiers as *the Bull Ring*. Here new drafts from Britain were taught the techniques of trench warfare by instructors who were known to their students as *Canaries* because of their yellow arm bands. George was to find, with some disgust, that many *Canaries* had never seen the front line. He described the shreiks, grunts and screams which these instuctors urged recruits to utter whilst thrusting bayonets into straw-filled sacks, as "rather silly." A detailed description of the regime at *Eat Apples* is to be found in Denis Winter's book *Death's men*.

Lance Corporal Morgan was to rejoin his Battalion on achieving his 19th birthday.

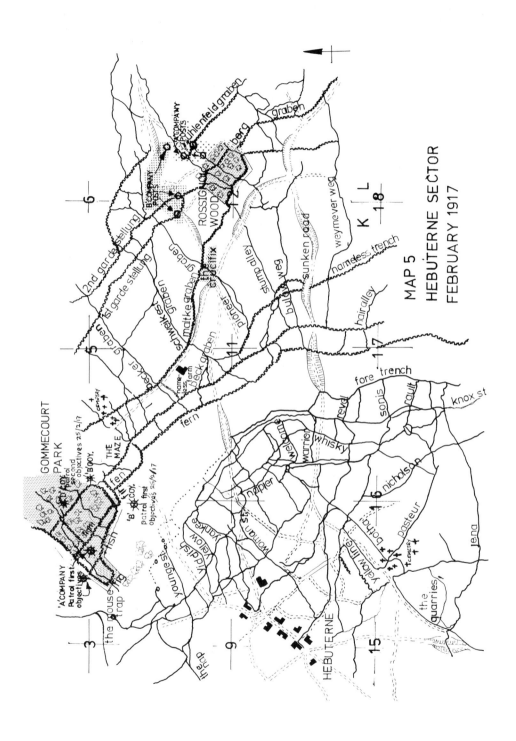

MAP 5
HEBUTERNE SECTOR
FEBRUARY 1917

No-man's land in front of Serre,1916. Imperial War Museum, *Neg. Q1910*

CHAPTER 6: GOMMECOURT PARK AND ROSSIGNOL WOOD

Next week the bloody Roll of Honour said
"Wounded and missing" - - - (That's the thing to do
When lads are left in shell holes dying slow,
With nothing but blank sky and wounds that ache,
Moaning for water till they know
It's night, and then it's not worth while to wake!)
Siegfried Sassoon

On February 21st, 1917, both battalions left Doullens and marched to Coigneux and hence into the trenches in the Hebuterne sector. The 16th Battalion occupied the L3 sub-sector with the 18th on their left flank in the L4 sub-sector. The 18th Battalion was now under the temporary command of Major C. W. Tilly of the 18th Durham Light Infantry, Lieutenant-Colonel H. F. G. Carter being hospitalised. Four days later Major Tilly became ill and Major A. W. Robinson assumed command.

On the 23rd February, the enemy began to evacuate his front line and fall back on to the Hindenburg line, a system of strong defences which straightened out his saliant between Arras and Vailly. The first indication that something unusual was taking place, on the opposite side of No-man's-land, was when smoke was observed rising from the German trenches at two points. Artillery was informed and a barrage of 18 pounder fire directed at these points for several hours. At 11.00 p.m. on February 24th, Brigade Headquarters wired that the enemy was thought to have left his front line trenches opposite V Corps, and ordered patrols out to investigate, including two patrols from the 18th Battalion.

Company commanders were ordered to Battalion Headquarters and briefed for these operations. Two platoons from 'A' Company, on the left, were to reconnoitre the tongue of the Gommmecourt saliant; two platoons from 'C' Company, on the right, were to search the south-west corner of the Park, at 'Fir trench'. These were the first objectives. Two platoons each from 'D' and 'B' Companies were to support and proceed to points beyond the third line of German trenches and well inside the Park. These were the second objectives. Patrols were instructed that, if the enemy line was found to be unoccupied, they were to push forward to their objectives with vigour. The 18th Battalion the Durham Light Infantry were ordered to move up in support to enable the exploitation of any gains. Zero hour was fixed at 5.00 a.m. on February 25th (see map 5).

The patrols moved off at the appointed hour but at 6.40 a.m. 'B' Company were reporting bomb and rifle fire on each flank. Shortly after this the enemy artillery became very active. Ten minutes later, a report was received from Captain J. R. Thornton of 'A' Company, saying that his patrol had reached its first objective but that he was not in touch with 'C' Company. A little later 2nd Lieutenant Hartman, of the 19th Divisional Artillery, reported at Battalion Headquarters that Captain Thornton had gained the tongue of the salient and that Lieutenant Sleigh, leading the other platoon from 'A' Company, was moving through the woods of Gommecourt Park. A party of ten of the enemy had been seen on the left and had been dispersed by Lewis gun fire. 2nd Lieutenant Hartman was instructed to rejoin Captain Thornton and tell him to press on to the second objective. Captain Thornton wrote later:

"I was in charge of No. 2 platoon and moved out from K3d 3.6 at 5.00 a.m. my objective being K2c2.9 to K3b 9.10. On moving into No-man's land a Very light was sent up from 'four tree SAP'. I moved north-east and entered a communication trench, at about K3b 9.5.10. Bombers were leading and we came into contact with an enemy post about K4c 9.0. The occupants of this post fled and we advanced to K4c 2.9.

I stayed in this trench for about 45 minutes during which time I sent a patrol up 'Fin' towards 'Field' and another along 'Fish' [these were code names for three German trenches in Gommecourt Park] to about 100 yards past the communication trench at K4c 7.6 without coming into contact with anyone. We were bombed from K4 2.2.05 and retaliated with bombs and claimed two hits. Shelling was heavy and as I could not get in touch with anyone I decided to return, leaving the enemy trench at about K4c 6.6, moving south of 'Yiddish'. I approached to a spot about K3d 9.8, from which smoke had been seen to issue for the last two days. This I found to be a burning dug-out, the wood around the entrance being charred."

2nd Lieutenant O. H. Staff

At 7.20 a.m., a runner arrived at Battalion Headquarters with a message from 2nd Lieutenant Priday, who was in charge of the reserve platoon of the right patrol, saying that he had met a platoon of 'A' Company who had been ordered to retire. He had put them in support in Z Hedge and gone on with No. 6 platoon. By 7.30 a.m. 'C' Company had reported the return of the platoon that had formed the right patrol and led by 2nd Lieutenant O. H. Staff who reported:

"I left Z Hedge as ordered at 5.35 a.m. and proceeded to my objective through our own wire, which had been cut. I found the enemy wire strong and had some trouble cutting through it. I entered the enemy trench and bombed five dug-outs. I

74

was met by a superior enemy force with a machine gun and, because my men's rifles were practically useless due to mud, I decided to withdraw."

The officer commanding 'C' Company was instructed to order the platoon forward again with support if necessary.

At 7.42 a.m., 'A' Company reported that Lieutenant Sleigh's platoon had returned on his orders but that he was not with them. About this time a heavy enemy bombardment developed shelling 'A' Company out of 'The Mouse Trap' opposite Gommecourt Park. The enemy was, by then, laying a heavy barrage on his own front line. On the fate of Lieutenant Sleigh, Captain Thornton wrote:

". . . Lieutenant Sleigh and No. 3 platoon followed behind me, I saw him enter at the same place (in the enemy line) as I had done. Apparently he continued north of 'Fin' and I heard bombing about 200 yards up. I did not see anything more of him. My casualties were nil."

Lieutenant Sleigh was subsequently posted missing, believed killed.

2nd Lieutenants Staff and Holt who had, by that time, submitted their reports to Battalion Headquarters were ordered out again with instructions to take the line and make every effort to hold it, but to return if this proved to be absolutely impossible. However, before this order could be executed, instructions were received from Brigade to withdraw all troops to their own lines. This decision was probably influenced by the fact that the 18th Battalion Durham Light Infantry was having difficulty in moving forward into support and, in fact, had not arrived by 7.47 a.m. The last patrol to return was No. 6 Platoon, led by 2nd Lieutenant N. H. Priday, who reported:

"No. 6 platoon left the line at 6.15 a.m. and on arrival at Z Hedge received a verbal message from the Officer commanding 'B' Company to the effect that I was to remain at Z Hedge in support. Here I met 2nd Lieutenant Hartman of the 19th Division Royal Field Artillery who told me that he had just returned from the first German line. Soon after this I saw No. 2 platoon arriving at the junction of 'Yiddish

2nd Lieutenant N. H. Priday

Street' and 'C' line. I learned that this platoon had been bombed out. This decided me to move my own platoon forward and bring No. 2 platoon into Z Hedge in support. This I effected and at 7.00 a.m., I despatched a message to the Officer commanding 'B' Company stating my intentions. I immediately moved forward in battle formation. A platoon of 'C' Company passed me here. They told me they had been bombed out and had lost direction. I explained what I was doing and continued my advance. I arrived at a point opposite K7c 5.7 and discovered two gaps in the wire. I immediately moved forward through these gaps into the Bosche line which I occupied at 7.30 a.m. I sent two runners to Z Hedge to bring forward No. 2 platoon under Sergeant Hustwick. On arrival of this party I pushed a point out about 50 yards inside Gommecourt Park and sent bombing parties along the trench on either flank, to try to get in touch with my flanks. These patrols returned, after half an hour's absence, stating that they had discovered no sign of anyone. I myself, with three men, pushed on into the Park to reconnoitre.

The mist was by this time, very thick so that I lost direction and with difficulty retraced my steps to my party. Whilst reconnoitring, three shots were fired in my direction from seemingly close at hand, but I could detect no sign of the enemy. On return I despatched a message to 'B' Company's Commanding Officer asking for reinforcements. Pending the arrival of these, I collected a quantity of enemy hand grenades, which I distributed amongst the men, at the same time explaining their use. At 9.00 a.m. my runners returned with a message stating that I was to retire as quickly as possible, which order I obeyed. During the hour and a half which I remained in the enemy's lines, no hostile movement was detected. All dug-outs in the vicinity were searched to no purpose and on retirement my party was not molested, but passed through a heavy hostile barrage, extending from the edge of our barbed wire entanglements to beyond Red line"

On the evening of the 26th, the 16th Battalion received orders to launch an attack on Rossignol Wood. The assault was to take place the following morning at 6.30 am, two companies forming the firing line with two companies in support. The two front companies were ordered to be clear of a line of posts on the Gommecourt-Puisieux Road at 6.30 am. Four, and later six, Lewis guns under the command of the Battalion Lewis gun officer, were positioned on the 'Sunken Road' to cover the advance and to fire upon any favourable targets. Major H. B. Byles, second in command, together with the Battalion signals, intelligence and medical officers took up a position at the Crucifix.

From there a line was laid to Battalion Headquarters in Woman Street. The extreme range ruled out a supporting barrage from the trench mortar battery.

The two companies, 'A' Company and 'C' Company, were clear of the enemy third line by 5.30 a.m. and deployed for the attack in No-man's-land, moving forward at about 6.00 am. with scouts well in advance.

The first report received from the scouts was that the southern edge of the Wood was occupied. The officer commanding 'C' Company, on the left, sent one platoon to move towards Pioneer Graben and occupy the high ground there. On reaching the trench they were met by an enemy counter-attack which drove them back towards the Crucifix. A bombing party under 2nd Lieutenant E. Crowther was immediately sent against the enemy and succeeded in driving them back about 180 yards after killing one and wounding several others. The party were able to establish blocks in Moltke Graben and Pioneer Graben and a bombing post at the junction of these trenches. The remainder of the company pushed forward, some men getting into the Wood whilst the rest dug themselves in in Stump Alley, and Pioneer Graben, south-west of the Crucifix, after losing some seven men killed and nine wounded in trying to move forward.

At 11.00 a.m., two platoons from the reserve companies were ordered forward to assist 'C' Company, who were not making much headway. This Company, although under heavy fire from 6.00 a.m. consolidated all the positions taken and stayed in them until relieved that night.

On the right, 'A' Company pushed forward into the southern edge of the Wood, three platoons entering by way of the trenches. The enemy immediately opened heavy fire upon them, with machine guns, infilading these trenches and killing or wounding almost their entire strength. 2nd Lieutenant Ashworth, who commanded No. 2 platoon, said in his report:

> "We came under heavy machine gun fire on reaching the crest of the hill about 600 yards from Rossignol Wood. I entered a communication trench and got my Lewis gun working."

He went on to say that the machine gun fire was from three directions and that they were also subjected to a light field gun barrage. Private W. Higgins, who went into action with Sergeant Farrar, No. 4 platoon, recalled:

> "We took cover as soon as the German machine guns opened fire. The heavy fire was kept up and it was practically impossible to move. My platoon was on the right and I was fourth man from the right. All the N.C.O.'s of my platoon were killed or wounded. I lay in the same position from where I could see about seven or eight men laying on the ground either killed or wounded. until about 4.00 p.m."

The Company's fourth, No. 3 platoon commanded by 2nd Lieutenant Tucker took cover in shell holes in the open and were able to rejoin the Battalion that night. Corporal E. Keighley who went into action with this platoon was to recall:

> "After we had crossed the third German line we came under heavy machine gun fire. I found that we were too crowded in the shell hole in which we had taken cover, so I took four of my men to find a better position. As I got to the top of the communication trench, two of my men were killed. I hung on

there for some time and, after about half an hour, 2nd Lieutenant Tucker came up and joined me."

Captain Armitage, the Company Commander, and Lieutenant Knight, were killed. Of the platoon commanders, Sergeant Farrar was killed and 2nd Lieutenants Ashworth and Tucker were wounded.

No messages were received from 'A' Company after 6.00 a.m. that morning until 2nd Lieutenant Tucker was able to report to Battalion Headquarters at 10.00 p.m. that night. Included in this Officer's Report, and referring to the wounded, are the following remarks:

"I saw a number of men laying about, out in the open, wounded and unable to get back. It was impossible to get stretcher bearers near them as the enemy was constantly sniping from the Wood. Men who were laying wounded were sniped at on making any attempt to reach cover, as the ground where they were was practically without shell holes and absolutely exposed to enemy fire, and snipers were firing incessantly."

In point of fact both Stump Alley and Bulow Weg were too wet and muddy for the use of stretchers. In addition they were exposed to enfilade fire from the Wood, so that these trenches could not be used for the evacuation of the wounded.

When darkness came, on the night of the 27th Lieutenant-Colonel Croydon relieved the two companies in the front line, at the Crucifix and the old German third line. Food and water together with ten boxes of ammunition and ten boxes of bombs were sent forward. At that time the Vickers and Lewis gun teams had been in their positions for 42 hours. During the attack the 16th Battalion had suffered 222 casualties, two officers and 64 other ranks had been killed, ten other ranks had died of their wounds, two officers and 83 other ranks had been wounded in action and 65 persons were missing. 'A' Company had suffered particularly heavily. As we have seen both the officers killed and both the officers wounded were from this company. In addition, the company lost 38 N.C.O.'s and other ranks killed, 35 N.C.O.'s and other ranks wounded whilst six N.C.O.'s and other ranks died of their wounds and 61 persons were posted missing. Among the N.C.O.'s who lost their lives were Company Sergeant Major Wilkinson, Sergeant Barnes and Sergeant Cockroft who had already lost two brothers in the campaign. All these men had joined the Battalion on its formation in 1914. Sergeant Nelson was the only Sergeant in 'A' Company to survive the day.

On the 28th, the 18th Battalion received orders to relieve the two companies of the 16th Battalion, and the two companies of the 15th Battalion on the right, from their new positions. Major Robinson also received verbal instructions that his Battalion would be required to attack Rossignol Wood on the morning of March 1st. These instructions were subsequently amended to the morning of March 2nd.

The relief moved off at 7.00 p.m. Lieutenant Morgan with one platoon from 'D' Company relieved the 16th Battalion from their positions in the Crucifix. Here, he set up a report centre and telephone, and established a party of Battalion bombers. Another platoon from 'D' Company relieved the 16th Battalion personnel in the old German line from K11d 3.7 to K11d 6.5. The remaining two platoons from this company relieved the 15th Battalion companies in their forward posts. 'A' and 'B' Companies established themselves in the old German 3rd and 2nd line from K11d 3.8 to K11d 8.0 and from K11c 8.9 to K11d 3.0. 'C' Company moved into the old German front line from K11c 5.7 to K11d 1.0. Battalion Headquarters was set up in Woman Street. The relief was completed by 12.00 midnight, the Battalion suffering seven casualties, wounded by shell fire.

The 16th Battalion were now relieved from support by the 13th Battalion the York and Lancaster Regiment and proceeded to a camp near Coigneux on the Courcellers Road.

Throughout the afternoon of the 1st, heavy smoke continued to rise from burning dug-outs in the Wood. From the early hours and throughout the day of the 2nd, the 18th Battalion maintained strong patrol activity. At mid-day the officer commanding 'B' Company was informed by Battalion Headquarters that it was intended to occupy the Wood "that night". Shortly before 1.00 p.m. 'D' Company reported that they had a patrol, consisting of an N.C.O. and two other men, probing up Stump Alley. They had been unable to reach the enemy line at the west corner of the Wood owing to a sniper, who had killed one of their men. A second N.C.O. patrol from 'D' Company had penetrated up Bulow Weg trench as far as the Wood, experiencing no opposition except sniping. The Wood end of the trench was found to be blocked with trees and wire. Another patrol was immediately sent out by the same route. Shortly before 3.00 p.m. a message was received from Brigade Headquarters which read: "Every endeavour will be made to enter Rossignol Wood and 1st Garde Stellung with strong patrols tonight. All ground gained will be held by strong posts and consolidated. . .'

By 5.30 p.m. the Battalion had a patrol working into the Wood at K12b 0.6 whilst another patrol was working up the continuation of Bulow Weg trench towards the Wood. A stronger patrol was waiting at the top of Bulow Weg for information from the advanced patrols. At 7.00 p.m. a patrol from 'B' Company moved out from the Crucifix with instructions to meet up with 2nd Lieutenant Priday and his platoon at the north-west corner of the Wood. The company moved out by platoons while 'A' Company moved up behind them. At 8.30 p.m. 'B' Company reported from the Sunken Road, near Stump Alley, that 2nd Lieutenant Priday and his men were in the Wood and had met with no opposition. Their remaining platoons were following up at 15 minute intervals. By 10.00 p.m. both 'A' and 'B' Companies were in the Wood with their Company Headquarters established at its edge in the extension of Bulow Weg. At 10.25 p.m. instructions were received from Brigade Headquarters ordering the Battalion to press on, after the Wood had been cleared, and establish a series of six posts to defend its approaches from the east. The Wood was to be lightly held owing to the possibility of heavy retaliatory shelling. The objectives of the 'Durhams' on their left, was 1st Garde Stellung from the junction of Lehmann Graben to the junction with Becker Graben thence working south-east along the trench to gain touch with the 18th Battalion at the point where the road intersected the trench. Posts were to be established at the junction of 1st Garde Stellung and the communication trench. At 11.50 p.m. advice was received from Brigade that patrols from the battalion on the right had been encountering serious opposition from K12d 7.8 and L7c 0.7 (some 200 and 500 yards to 'A' Company's right) since 7.30 p.m. The message from this battalion, the 6th Battalion the Wiltshire Regiment, continued: ". . . am endeavouring to obtain possession of the Berg Graben between these points to make a flank attack."

By this time 'B' Company were consolidating a line a little to the north of the Wood, assisted by a platoon from 'A' Company. They had established the three strong points shown on map 5. 'A' Company had one and a half platoons at the north-east neck of the Wood and had established three strong points there, also shown on map 5. A further one and a half platoons were in the Wood's south-west corner and in the first 200 yards of Berg Graben. Six prisoners had been taken. By 12.40 a.m. the Wiltshires had occupied the rest of the Berg Graben.

Shortly after 5.00 a.m. the 18th Durham Light Infantry reported that one of their patrols, moving along 1st Garde Stellung, had met with heavy opposition and considered that the trench was strongly held. At 11.00 am. a message arrived from 2nd Lieutenant Bradford, of the Durhams, who reported:

"I am quite near the barrier at the junction of Pioneer Graben and 1st Garde Stellung. Have patrols out myself. About 100 of the enemy have been seen in the vicinity, wiring and working on the parapet. His wire is very thick and deep and the barricade is the same also. He has evidently seen some of our men, also heard bombs thrown because he is now manning his line. The line is strongly held and, owing to the depth and thickness of the wire, chances of getting through are small."

When this information was passed to the Durhams, their Commanding Officer asked Major Robinson to render any assistance possible to help 2nd Lieutenant Bradford clear up the situation. He left it to the Major to decide upon and carry out what operations he considered necessary to help the Lieutenant in achieving his objectives. Two patrols, one of Durhams and one from the 18th Battalion were immediately ordered out to ascertain the strength of the enemy. Both patrols reported the 1st Garde Stellung at point 70 and probably the 2nd Garde Stellung at point 82 to be strongly held. After consultations with Brigade, Major Robinson decided to attack these strong points. His operational order read:

Major Robinson

"At 5 p.m. the Infantry of Keel (the 18th Battalion West Yorks) and the Infantry of Deck (the 18th Battalion the Durham Light Infantry) will get into battle formation extended order as close to the barrage as possible. At 5.10 p.m. the Infantry will rush the positions at K6c 82 and K6c 02, (these positions were, in fact, strong points). Before 5.00 p.m. the Infantry of Keel and Deck must not be within 250 yards of the triangle formed by the neck of the north-west saliant of the wood and a line from K12b 2.4 to K12b 3.6."

The operation was carried out with dash and vigour and, by 6.10 p.m. 'B' Company had reported that 1st Garde Stellung had been entered, that 20 prisoners had been captured and that the position was being consolidated. Captain Thornton was reported wounded. At 7.27 p.m. Brigade signalled: "Wire directly you are in a satisfactory position for relief to commence. When stating this, position of all your posts, supporting platoons and Company Headquarters must be forwarded before sanction is given for relief to take place".

The dispositions of the companies was then relayed to Brigade but, before requesting relief, Major Robinson visited all posts to check their positions stated (strong points K6c 9.1 and trench K6c 8.2). He led men to their correct positions and saw them consolidating their posts before moving on to inspect other posts. After visiting all the posts in the Garde Stellung and Rossignol Wood, and requesting the 13th Battalion York and Lancaster Regiment to relieve two platoons of 'C' Company in 2nd Garde Stellung, he returned to Battalion Headquarters and

Frank Burn on active service, September 1916.

reported his situation to Brigade as being "quite satisfactory for relief."

By 12.30 a.m. on the 4th, relief had been completed by the 13th York and Lancaster Regiment, except for the two platoons of 'C' Company who were still busy consolidating their positions. These platoons were relieved at 2.30 a.m. The Battalion then moved to Hebuterne where they remained until the afternoon. Then they marched to billets in Bayencourt. The casualties suffered by the Battalion during these operations were described as light.

Captain J. R. Thornton was carried out of the trenches by his orderly and company runner, Private Frank Burn. The two, had been inseparable since Festubert. When he attended a Company Commander's course at Condett, the Captain had taken Frank with him as his servant. Frank was at that time, under the age of 19 and, therefore, not allowed to be employed in the trenches. Captain Thornton, happily, recovered from his wounds. The two were able to continue their comradeship in later years through the Bradford Pals Old Comrades' Association. Captain Thornton was, for many years, President of the Association, whilst Frank Burn held the office of Chairman until the Association was disbanded in 1979.

Lieutenant Norman Priday was awarded a Military Cross for his courage and initiative.

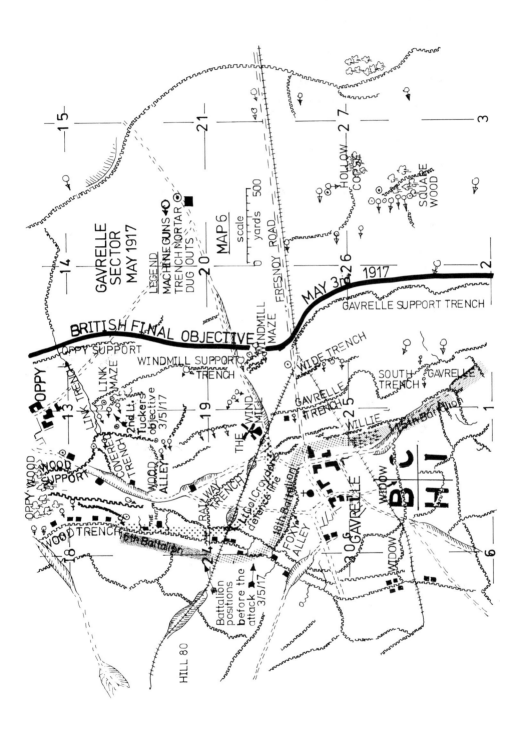

GAVRELLE SECTOR MAY 1917

LEGEND
MACHINE GUNS
TRENCH MORTAR
DUG OUTS

MAP 6

scale
0   500
yards

BRITISH FINAL OBJECTIVE

MAY 3rd 1917

GAVRELLE SUPPORT TRENCH

OPPY SUPPORT

WINDMILL SUPPORT
TRENCH

WINDMILL
MAZE

WIDE TRENCH

SOUTH
TRENCH

GAVRELLE

OPPY

LINK TRENCH

LINK
MAZE

2nd Lt.
Tucker's
objective
3/5/17

WIND
MILL

GAVRELLE
TRENCH

WILLIE

VIII BN. DILLON

OPPY WOOD

WOOD
SUPPORT

COVERED
TRENCH

WOOD
ALLEY

THE

RAILWAY
TRENCH

Lt.Col.Croyden's
defensive line

18th Battalion

WIDOW

GAVRELLE

B

C

H

I

WOOD TRENCH

THE HUT

16th Battalion

FOX
ALLEY

GAVRELLE

WIDOW

Battalion
positions
before the
attack 3/5/17

HILL 80

FRESNOY ROAD

HOLLOW

SQUARE
WOOD

No-man's land in front of Serre,1916. Imperial War Museum, *Neg. Q1910.*

CHAPTER 7: GAVRELLE AND OPPY WOOD

Men jostle and climb to meet the bristling fire
Lines in grey, muttering faces, masked with fear,
They leave their trenches, going over the top,
While time ticks blank and busy on their wrists,
And hope with furtive eyes and grappling fists
Flounders in the mud. O Jesus make it stop!
Siegfried Sassoon.

Towards the end of March, 1917, the 93rd Brigade moved back to the Bethune area. The 18th Battalion were in billets in Feuillade Barracks in the town of Bethune, whilst the 16th Battalion were accommodated in Neauvry. A brief period of cleaning up, training, route marching, etc., made a welcome break from life in the trenches.

On the 28th April, the 93rd Brigade was ordered back to the Arras front, where they relieved the 63rd Naval Division in the vicinity of Gavrelle. On arrival in this sector, the Brigade was immediately concentrated in the forward area. The 16th Battalion occupied the left sub-sector. On their right the 15th Battalion held Gavrelle. The 18th Battalion went into the support positions with 'B' Company on Hill 80, the remaining companies in the support trenches some 400 yards west of Gavrelle.

The beginning of the month had seen the opening of the Allied spring offensive. The British Armies had driven the enemy from Vimy Ridge and broken his line east of Arras. The positions which both battalions now occupied had only recently been held by the Germans.

By the end of April the French offensive, in the south, was running into difficulties. On May 3rd, to take some of the pressure off their allies, the British First and Third Armies struck towards Fresnoy. The 31st Division took part with the 2nd Division on their left and the 9th Division on their right. The 92nd Brigade attacked on the Division's left, the 93rd Brigade on the right. The objectives of the 31st Division were the German 1st and 2nd lines. These are shown, in so far as they effect the 93rd Brigade, on map no. 6.

2nd Lieutenant R. W. Clarkson of the 18th Battalion recalled: "Before going up to the line a day before the attack, each officer was received by Colonel Carter, who wished luck to him and his men. Everyone was in good heart and determined not to let himself and others down."

2nd Lieutenant R. W. Clarkson

For hours there had been almost continuous shelling by both sides and the first job was to advance an hour before zero in order to man the direction tapes at intervals extending over about 200 yards. This was done without interruption from the enemy.

The Brigade lined up for the attack with the 16th Battalion on the left. Then the 18th Battalion, divided into two halves, one half on the right of the 16th and one half on the left of the 15th Battalion who formed the Brigade's right flank. The three battalions were each to attack on a double company front, and in four waves. The 18th were lined up in half companies in the order, left to right, 'A', 'D', 'C', 'B'. Thus 'A' and 'D' Companies operated in conjunction with the 16th and 'C' and 'B' Companies with the 15th Battalion.

The 16th Battalion were assembled with two platoons of 'D' Company on the right and two platoons of 'C' Company on the left in the first wave. The second wave was made up from the remaining platoons of these companies. 'B' Company, including George Morgan, now a Sergeant, formed the third wave and 'A' Company the fourth.

The officers of the 16th Battalion who went forward with the attacking waves in 'A' Company were Captain Illingworth, 2nd Lieutenant Bantock, 2nd Lieutenant Cowell, 2nd Lieutenant L. Ashworth and 2nd Lieutenant Tucker, the Battalion Bombing Officer, who, with a party of Regimental bombers and rifle grenadiers, had been detailed to deal with the enemy strong points in, and around, the Link Maze. In 'B' Company the officers were Captain Ashworth, 2nd Lieutenant Platnauer, 2nd Lieutenant Cook. In 'C' Company they were Lieutenant Crowther, 2nd Lieutenant Parker, 2nd Lieutenant Greville. In 'D' Company they were Captain P. L. Parker, 2nd Lieutenant Barltrop, and 2nd Lieutenant Bantock, who was attached to this company for the operation.

With Lieutenant-Colonel Croydon in Battalion Headquarters were 2nd Lieutenant Stanley, acting as Adjutant, Lieutenant Barrow, the Battalion Intelligence Officer, 2nd Lieutenant J. Johnson, the Signals Officer, 2nd Lieutenant Bartlett, the Artillery Officer and 2nd Lieutenant Bentock, acting as Liaison Officer with the 18th Battalion the East Yorkshire Regiment.

Artillery methods had improved since the Battle of the Somme. New techniques included the 'creeping barrage' where infantry advanced behind a moving wall of exploding shells; that is, if they were able to differentiate between their own barrage and that of the enemy. The technique was to be used on this occasion.

The Brigade attack itself was divided into two halves, the right, or southern attack, and the left, or northern attack. The barrage on the left was only to move, or creep, at a rate of 100 yards in four minutes so as to conform with the brigade on the left who were to attack Oppy. The barrage on the right was to creep at the rate of 100 yards in two minutes. This was to conform with the brigade on the right. Zero hour was fixed for 3.45 a.m.

At 2 a.m. the enemy laid a heavy barrage on the British front line which lasted 20 minutes. It caught both battalions as they were preparing to leave the protection of their trenches to line up on the assembly guide tapes laid the night before. (Unfortunately, the Battalion's war diaries make no mention of the gallantry of, nor of the casualties suffered by, the officers and men who laid these direction tapes.) Many 18th Battalion men were killed or wounded. In his report on the attack, Lieutenant-Colonel Carter described how no one hung back but climbed out unhesitatingly and fearlessly into a bristling fire, in some cases treading over the bodies of their dead comrades to do so.

At 3.00 a.m. in response to an S.O.S. from Oppy Wood, the enemy laid a heavy barrage lasting 17 minutes on the British front line.

Promptly at 3.45 a.m. the British bombardment began and the three battalions rose to their feet and moved forward, close to the barrage, extended in good order. Unfortunately for them, No-man's-land was bathed in bright moonlight.

At 3.49 a.m. an intense enemy barrage was directed at the entire British front, accompanied by heavy machine gun and rifle fire from the left flank and immediate front. The artillery barrage was to last until 12.00 noon.

By 4.00 a.m. the 16th Battalion's first waves had reached their first objectives, passing through the enemy wire, which was sparse, without difficulty. As the barrage lifted, they advanced into the enemy trench, which they found to be only lightly held and experienced a minimum of opposition. Prisoners were taken and the first wave set about consolidating the trench whilst the following waves pressed on, behind the barrage, to the second objective. The enemy were seen to leave this position in large numbers, retiring in disorder and suffering heavy casualties from fire brought to bear upon them from the advancing troops. This trench was occupied, but it was then that Captain Parker, leading 'D' Company, realised that the companies on his left had not come up. Steps were taken to consolidate the trench, which was very shallow. Digging proved to be difficult due to the chalky nature of the ground. Lewis gun posts were pushed well out.

In most cases the 18th's 'left half battalion' had reached their first and second objectives. However, heavy machine gun fire had sadly depleted their ranks by the time they had reached the second objective. There was some considerable loss of direction, possibly because of the fact that two consecutive casualties in a line, left the men 24 yards apart. On the right, however, the 'right half battalion' did not get much further than their first objective. In one or two places they were held up by wire but in the main they were wiped out by machine gun fire

Corporal W. Palframan

before reaching the first line of German trenches. Many of these machine guns were firing from unmarked strong points, often consisting of shafts dug out from the bottom of large shell holes and leading to emplacements that opened out into the crest or the back of the hilly ground. Corporal Palframan of 'B' Company, who was second in command of No. 8 'Moppers-up' platoon, found such a post just past the Windmill and in front of the enemy line. He reported it as a very deep hole, about 20 feet deep, and funnel shaped. He got two prisoners out of it but elected not to investigate further. He therefore bombed it. Corporal Palframan was awarded a Distinguished Service Medal and, later, was to be commissioned in the field.

Here let 2nd Lieutenant Clarkson take up his story:

"'B' Company, including my platoon, formed part of the first wave on the right. Before zero hour advanced my platoon left the trenches to line up on the tapes which directed the attack, half left, towards the supposed enemy line, so far as the disjointed front was known. Guesswork, mostly.

At 3.45 a.m. zero hour came in as a quiet, dark dawn. Our only orders were to advance behind the creeping barrage which, at that time moved slightly forward, at the same time the enemy barrage intensified, and would continue to do so until the German trenches were reached. We had no idea how far this would be. It was expected that our artillery would have made their front line uninhabitable so whatever trench we entered was to be made as defendable as possible. The expectation was that the second wave would pass through us to the second objective. All 'according to the book'! My platoon was depleted to about 20 including a Lewis gun section of four men carrying guns and ammunition. I remember that this seemed a bit weak for an advance attacking a line of about 200 yards.

'What', thought this young civilian Subaltern, 'is one supposed to do now?' Twenty men stretched over 150/200 yards in the gloom carrying bayonets at the ready, all trying to keep a straight line, not knowing what to expect, hoping for an abandoned front line but, in all probability, trenches full of quick-firing enemy. A Subaltern should be in front of his *Pals,* first thought he to himself. Secondly, he should show a good example (God help me!) Perhaps talking in a loud voice, encouraging and directing. They may then know where you are. (But the noise was deafening - How could they hear what was being said?) The walking was anything but good, plenty of obstacles to step on, still dark before dawn, air thick with smoke and bursting shells and no view of one's troops except for the one or two on one's left and right, certainly no more. One remembers shouting at several figures:

Don't bunch! Spread out.

Where are the N.C.O.'s? Doing what they can to keep things going but none to be seen in the gloom. One remembers calling to Batman Riley (a good chap): 'Riley, where are you?' 'Here, Sir,' someone replies. Then, after about ten minutes . . . . WHAM! something hard hit on the right side somewhere and caused one to tumble to the ground. No real pain and finding walking was still possible, had to catch up with the platoon who must be somewhere in front by then. One was in the back now, instead of in the front. Finally, the light becoming a bit better, a German trench in front so jumped in hoping to find men of the platoon. What now! Wound bleeding a lot but not much pain. Found two dead Germans in the large Strong Point and about 12 of our men from different platoons all of whom were wounded pretty badly except one who kept a look out. No one strong enough to turn the trench the other way round [*to prepare the trench against counter-attack].* Tried to keep the injured in good trim and hoped to find the second wave troops arriving to re-inforce. None, of-course, arrived and, at this point, now daylight and less firing, a friend, Lieutenant Daws, slipped into the trench having lost touch with his own lot. He'd managed to get this far without being wounded and realising our situation decided to try and get back to Battalion Headquarters which I gather he did.

I wrote a message and entrusted it to my only active soldier but I am certain he did not manage to make it.

To one's surprise a German Feltfabel arrived in our trench.

'So,' one thought 'we have got a prisoner!' He was not carrying a gun but no doubt he had one whereas I was carrying one before being wounded but I now found that the shrapnel which I had stopped had severed my lanyard and dropped the revolver in No-man's land! We were, of-course, at his mercy. He approached me being the only one showing any authority although didn't recognise me as an officer being, as usual, in private's uniform. He made it clear his reason for visiting us in daylight was to see what had happened to his own men. He was a civilised man and before leaving us he found my first aid kit and tied me up [dressed the wounds] and made me understand that we would be taken to a dressing station as soon as it became dusk. And so it happened. I just managed a short walk and on the way I saw Norman Priday on a stretcher with leg wounds. We had only a minute or so to talk together . . .And so ended my association with the Bradford Pals."

Private Page of 'A' Company went forward with No. 3 platoon in the third wave. They got into the second line where they became mixed with 'B' Company. Lieutenant Robinson of that company was there, busily trying to service a German machine gun. However, there was no one on their left. They began to dig in but were sniped at from all sides and fired on by machine guns. They could see the Germans massing for a counter attack and extending around them. Then they saw the 16th Battalion retiring.

Sergeant Tidmarsh of 'C' Company and the 3rd wave got as far as the enemy wire, about 30 yards in front of the first objective. The wire was uncut and about four yards thick. They drove the enemy from his trench but, because of the uncut wire, they found themselves outflanked and had to retire.

Sergeant Calverley led a platoon from 'B' Company in the fourth wave. His objective was to make a strong point some 50 yards in front of the Windmill. The Sunken Road, just past the railway was manned by the enemy. There were some dug outs there and a machine gun post, although the latter appeared to have been knocked out. A big gap existed between the Sergeant's party and 'C' Company and it seemed to him that his own company had gone too far to the right and that they had become mixed up with 'C' Company. He got his platoon into the German first line where about seven of his men, together with the Company Sergeant Major, began to work their way along the trench. Then they saw on their left 'A' Company retiring with their arms slung. They were being followed, at a distance of about 180 yards, by a party of Germans who were firing on them. Since 'A' Company were retiring, Sergeant Calverley was forced to do the same. It was as they were going back that the Company Sergeant Major was killed.

At 6.13 a.m. runners brought a verbal message from Company Sergeant Major Nicholson, of Tarran's company, saying that all officers were missing, the majority of the men were casualties and that he himself was wounded. They had reached their first objective but whilst making towards their second, machine guns firing on them from each flank had caused heavy losses.

Private Tarran of 'D' Company said that his company had followed the barrage to within 20 yards of the German trench. There they came under a cross fire from two machine guns, one firing from the main road and the other from a ditch. Although they reached the first objective the first two waves had been practically wiped out. He crawled into a shell hole and, finding no other men there, returned to his own lines.

2nd Lieutenant Harris of 'A' Company said later that after the barrage commenced, the company had become somewhat disorganized and, after crossing the road, 16th and 18th Battalion men and those of different companies had become mixed together. A great number had congregated in a trench and he himself, together with a brother officer of the 16th Battalion, went over to their right and took ten prisoners. His companion then received information that they were being surrounded on both flanks. A party of the 16th Battalion appeared on their left. He took his party, and his prisoners, across to join them. The officer in charge of this party, presumably Captain Parker, told him he had better report at Battalion Headquarters. This he did, arriving with about 20 men and a Sergeant.

Captain Ashforth of 'B' Company, 16th Battalion, followed 'D' Company whilst his other two platoons led by 2nd Lieutenant Platnauer followed 'C' Company. After crossing the Sunken Road his men came under fire from several enemy posts, which they disposed of, but at this point found that they were out of touch with the battalion on the right. They reached the first objective at 4.00 a.m. and crossed over, advancing onto the second line which they took without difficulty. At this point, contact was established with both Captain Parker and Captain Illingworth.

An unknown N.C.O. and three other ranks, probably some of 2nd Lieutenant Platnauer's men, found themselves pinned down in a shell hole in front of an enemy post. From the post came a German who attempted to throw a grenade into their midst. He was immediately cut down by four simultaneous shots from the shell hole. This man was almost immediately replaced by a second grenadier who was also cut down. This procedure continued until some eight men had fallen before the party's rifles. When no others appeared the N.C.O., covered by his comrades, crawled out to investigate. He found that the entire garrison of the post lay shot dead in front of his shell hole. Had these gallant men launched a simultaneous bomb attack, the result for the N.C.O.'s party would have been less fortunate.

At about 5.00 a.m. a party of about 100 of the enemy was seen approaching Captain Parker's positions from half right and in three waves. At first it was thought that the party was coming to surrender and they were waved on. The enemy, however, immediately opened fire. This fire was returned with Lewis guns and rifles causing many casualties and forcing the enemy to fall back in disorder. Shortly afterwards Captain Duckitt, of the 18th Battalion, came up into 'C' Company positions with four men. At 5.30 a.m. the enemy opened up with heavy machine gun and rifle fire from the rear, killing Sergeant Manley, wounding 2nd Lieutenant Ashworth, and making digging and consolidation of the newly won positions difficult. By 7.30 a.m., however, the trench was in good condition for defence in the centre but still very shallow on the flanks. At this time Captain Parker estimated that he had 100 men with him. Very shortly after this the enemy began to advance in strength from the front, with waves in extended order leading, and massed in the rear. The intensity of machine gun fire and sniping from the flank and the rear was considerably increased. It was about this time that Captain Illingworth was reported killed.

As the enemy waves came down the ridge and onto the front a heavy Lewis gun and rifle fire was directed against them, causing heavy casualties. Sergeant Agar, in charge of 'A' Company Lewis gun, estimated that he entirely wiped out a party of roughly 50 men, advancing in file and at a range of 50 to 60 yards. At this stage the enemy showed an inclination to surrender freely but, as the situation on the flanks became apparent, their morale recovered and the attack developed. Captains Parker, Ashworth and Duckitt held a short conference and, taking into consideration the fact that both flanks were open, and that, therefore, they would very soon be surrounded, they decided to retire to their own lines, and this from the left. The order "Lead on from the left" was given, but there was no exit from the left. So the order was given to withdraw from the trench by the rear. Practically all 'A' Company's casualties were suffered during the withdrawal, owing to heavy machine gun fire from all sides, and included 2nd Lieutenant Cowell who was hit between the shoulders.

Shortly after the barrage had started Lieutenant-Colonel Croydon had discovered that the battalion on his left had been held up, causing the gap referred to previously. He immediately ordered his adjutant, 2nd Lieutenant Stanley, to organize two bombing parties, composed of Headquarters, Signallers, Runners, and an Artillery liaison officer, to block the trench. Some few minutes later a party of the enemy were seen coming down Wood Trench from Oppy. 2nd Lieutenant Stanley immediately jumped over the parapet with a party of bombers and bombed the enemy party from behind, thereby cutting off their line of retreat and compelling some fourteen of them to surrender. At that moment some men from the 10th east Yorks came doubling down the trench saying that they had been driven out of their positions by the enemy. Lieutenant-Colonel Croydon halted them and put them out in shell holes to the left and to the right, thus making a strong line of defence. In the meantime 2nd Lieutenant Stanley had taken out another party of bombers and worked around the back of the enemy, some of them surrendered immediately. It was then that 2nd Lieutenant Stanley was wounded. During this period, stragglers from various units who were coming back, were organized and directed into a defensive line by the Colonel. A bombing party with a Lewis gun had been established up the trench under the command of the Intelligence Officer together with the Signal's Officer, stragglers and battalion observers.

Lieutenant-Colonel Croydon was now able to get his wounded to the rear and to request reinforcements. The time was now 5.05 a.m. Lieutenant Colonel Carter, hearing of the request for assistance, visited Lieutenant-Colonel Croyden's Headquarters to confer. He reported the situation to Brigade as follows:

"16th West Yorks holding B24d 6.5. Apparently some of our men retiring from trench leading from railway towards Oppy Wood in first objective, about C13c or C19a. Enemy look as if he will counter-attack from Oppy Wood, and is putting a pretty heavy barrage on the eastern flank of our trenches between Sunken Road near old 16th West Yorks Headquarters and the railway (i.e. B30a and railway B24d). Hill 80 should be held at once so as to prevent enemy turning our flanks, and if possible a machine gun or two placed between between Hill 80 and our trenches along the railway. Situation on our right not known regarding holding of original trenches, because matters are so disorganized and the trenches so badly damaged that it is quite possible that the enemy will counter-attack and try to regain the whole of Gavrelle. Our original line should be held at all costs, and unless more troops are available, a further attack cannot be made. Machine guns and Lewis guns will be wanted but above all, Hill 80 should be held."

The enemy did not show any inclination to attack Lieutenant Colonel Carter's defence line in force but began to retire slowly towards Oppy. Heavy casualties were inflicted on them by Lewis gun and rifle fire. However the enemy artillery then brought a barrage of 5.9's and 8.0's to bear, making the position untenable. The Colonel, therefore, decided to withdraw his small force to a better position, in rear of the railway, which had been selected by Lieutenant-Colonel Carter. The force went back to their new positions two men at a time, where they dug themselves in on a 70 yard front. On arrival in his new positions Lieutenant-Colonel Croydon was struck on the helmet and knocked down by a shell burst, leaving him concussed. He was taken to the dug-out of Lieutenant-Colonel Carter who assumed temporary command of the situation. However, after a period of about four hours rest, Lieutenant Colonel Croydon was able to resume his command. By then, reinforcements from the Durham Light Infantry were beginning to arrive in his positions.

Many men were killed and a great number wounded during the retirement, owing to the trenches being blown in, thus providing excellent targets for the enemy machine gunners who constantly fired from the right and from the front. Later in the day an attempt was made to regain the original positions but it was found to be impossible to get beyond the railway until after dark, due to the continuous hostile bombardment, snipers and machine gun fire. At 3.15 p.m. Brigade ordered that a composite battalion be formed from the survivors of the 16th and 18th Battalions and placed under the command of Lieutenant-Colonel Croydon. All available 18th Battalion troops (less Battalion Headquarters) were put in the charge of 2nd Lieutenants Dams and Harris and placed at the disposal of Lieutenant-Colonel Croydon.

Later in the day Lieutenant-Colonel Croydon's small force began to work their way back to their original positions. They finally achieved these objectives on the following day. In addition to the men from the 18th Battalion, the force now comprised men from the East Yorkshire Regiment, 18th Battalion the Durham Light Infantry, The King's Own Yorkshire Light Infantry, the Royal Engineers, the Machine Gun Corps, the Light Trench Mortar Batteries and, of course, the 16th Battalion. About 50 prisoners were taken during the operation but many of these were killed by their own artillery fire as they made their way to the rear areas.

There seems little doubt that the Colonel's action thwarted the enemy's attempt to cut off all the troops who had gone forward during the attack. Had he not remained at the position taken up, the War Diary argues, many men would have been taken prisoner as they came back that way.

The casualties suffered among the 16th Battalion's officers on the 3rd were:

Captain O. Illingworth, 'A' Comp	Reported killed in action
2nd Lieut A. H. Barltrop,'A' Comp	Wounded in action
2nd Lieut F. T. Cowell, 'A' Comp	Wounded in action
2nd Lieut J. L. Stanley, 'C' Comp	Wounded in action
2nd Lieut E. Crowther, 'C" Comp	Missing,believed wounded
2nd Lieut L.M.Platnauer,'B' Comp	Wounded, and missing
2nd Lieut G. L. Tucker, 'A' Comp	Missing
2nd Lieut L. Ashworth, 'A' Comp	Missing
2nd Lieut E. G. Bantock,'A' Comp	Missing
2nd Lieut N. Parker, 'C' Comp	Missing
2nd Lieut D. O. Greville,'C' Comp	Missing

The casualties for other ranks for this day were:

	'A'	'B'	'C'	'D'
Killed in action	5	1	4	8
Missing	24	33	90	29
Missing believed killed			1	
Missing believed wounded			3	
Wounded and missing	1			
Wounded but still at post		5		
Wounded in action	25	23	19	32
Total	55	62	117	69

Total casualties for the day were, therefore, 11 officers and 303 other ranks.

The War Diaries do not contain a list of casualties suffered by the 18th Battalion on this day but, from the foregoing account the reader will, no doubt, conclude that they were equally heavy.

Lieutenant-Colonel Croydon's report on the operation ends with the following statement:

"I consider that the following lessons are learnt from these operations.

(1)   The chief thing I noticed in the recent operations were first, the preliminary bombardments in my opinion are unnecessary.

(2)   Atmospheric conditions should be studied. Owing to bright moonlight the enemy saw our men forming up in No-man's-land, which caused an S.O.S. signal from Oppy Wood followed by a barrage.

(3)   Length of front was, in my opinion, too great, and caused the line to be very weak and extension great.

(4)   Reserves should be brought up into the line which the attacking party vacates, and kept there for any emergency. They could also be used for filling up the attacking line where seen to be thin, or to deliver a counter attack.

(5)   A Staff Officer should be detailed to view the ground previous to operations as battalions vary in strength and maps are not always accurate.

(6)   A Battalion Commander should always have a small reserve at his disposal to enable him to meet any emergency.

(7)   Owing to the weakness of the force that reached the final objective it was impossible to consolidate. Strength and depth should be considered.

(8)   The concentration of Artillery fire on known strong points and their immediate vicinity."

The early hours of the 4th were marked by the enemy acting in a very nervous manner, Verey lights and occasional S.O.S.'s appearing along the whole front. At 3.10 a.m. he put down a barrage along the British front line trench and around Gavrelle, the duration of which was about 20 minutes. His registration in the vicinity of the railway, and the point where it crossed the trench at B24b, was described as being "very accurate." Hostile machine guns maintained a constant bickering from around B18d 7.8. British artillery retaliated along the whole front during the night, systematically shelling the enemy front and support trenches, Hollow Copse and Fresnes. Between 9.00 a.m. and noon, artillery activity decreased. Little enemy movement was seen with the exception of some activity south of Oppy and near Linkburn. At 9.00 a.m. the 'block' at B18d 45.50 was found to be occupied by a party of extremely alert German troops who challenged any approach with a shower of hand grenades.

The positions occupied by the 16th and 18th Battalions now ran from near the Windmill to B24d, then to B24d 3.7, B24 6.3.0. and then northwards to B18d 4.5. The Battalions also occupied a newly constructed trench from B24c 9.5 to B24c 7.3.

On the night of the 4th/5th both Battalions were relieved by the 14th York and Lancaster Regiment and proceeded to a camp at St. Catherine, near Arras.

During the 5th, 6th and 7th May, both battalions rested. With the exception of cleaning up clothing and kit, there were no parades. Each battalion was reorganized into two companies, designated No. 1 Company and No. 2 Company, which gives some indication of battalion strengths at that time.

On the 8th, the 93rd Brigade received orders to relieve the Gavrelle sector, the 16th being detailed as 'Brigade Reserve' and relieving the 13th York and Lancaster Regiment in a system of trenches west of Railway Cutting whilst the 18th Battalion occupied the support trenches. On the night of the 16th both Battalions moved forward and took over the trenches occupied by the 18th Durham Light Infantry who were to make an attack on Gavrelle trench. Much work was done by the 16th Battalion in strengthening and deepening the trench north and south of the Gavrelle-Fresnes Road with a view to making a good taking off trench for the Durhams. This activity did not go unnoticed by the enemy who directed a continuous barrage of 4.2 inch and 5.9 inch shells on to the front line. The work was not therefore completed without casualties. The Battalion lost three killed and eight wounded on the 12th and two killed and 13 wounded on the 13th.

May 17th found the 16th Battalion in the support trenches Jewel and Joyous as Brigade reserve. The 18th Battalion had a half battalion in the support trenches and a half battalion in 'Willie', the front line trench, from a point adjacent to Gavrelle Cemetery to where it crossed the road at I1b 2.7. The latter half were to be 'in support' to the 18th Battalion the Durham Light Infantry who were to attack Gavrelle trench during the hours of darkness.

At 12.30 a.m. on May 18th, the barrage began and the 'Durhams' went forward. Three parties of that Battalion actually reached their objectives, the two smaller groups were driven out immediately although the third party, numbering about 40 men, stayed in the German trench for about 30 minutes before they too were driven out. The company attacking on the south side were met by a bomb barrage and failed to reach their objective. By noon the attack had been declared a failure.

Both battalions were now relieved by units of the 63rd Naval Division on the evening of the 19th, the 16th moving into a camp near Roclincourt and the 18th to a camp near Ecurie.

From this date until the 27th, both battalions were mainly employed in the provision of working and carrying parties. On that day the 16th Battalion moved to billets at Maroeuil whilst the 18th Battalion marched to hutments in Bray. The 16th's departure for Maroeuil was marked by a grenade, accidentally thrown into an incinerator during 'last minute clearing up', exploding and wounding 11 men. Both battalions now enjoyed a brief respite of a few days which were employed in battalion training, musketry, etc. Sufficient replacements were received to enable both battalions to be reorganized into four companies. News was received on June 5th that the courage of 16th Battalion personnel had been recognised by the following awards: Captain Parker - Military Cross, 2nd Lieutenant J. L. Stanley - Distinguished Service Order, Private Hallam - Distinguished Conduct Medal.

On June 9th, both battalions began another spell in the trenches of the Gavrelle Sector. The weather was wet and rain storms on the 11th badly flooded the trenches making them, in many places, impassable. Considerable labour was needed in clearing them, digging sump holes and laying duck boards to render movement possible.

The period was marked by a great deal of patrol activity by both battalions. On the night of the 18th one such patrol included Frank Burn. After spending some time studying the antics of an enemy seen signalling from his parapet with a red lamp, they returned with a Lewis gun which they had found in front of the wire. Even in recent years this gun has proved to be the source of much inter-battalion banter. Frank Burn always maintained that the gun was the property of the 16th Battalion who had left it there during the attack on the 3rd May. Needless to say, this has always been hotly denied.

On the night of the 23rd June, while the 18th Battalion was resting in bivouacs behind Railway Cutting, a long range gun shelled the vicinity of the encampment. One shell fell on the orderly room tent, killing three clerks and wounding Lieutenant-Colonel Carter.

During June, news was received that Captain Illingworth, reported killed in action, Lieutenant Crowther and 2nd Lieutenants Ashworth, Bentock, Barker and Tucker, reported missing since the attack on May 3rd., all of the 16th Battalion, were prisoners-of-war in Germany.

July opened with the Brigade still in the Gavrelle Sector and maintaining strong patrol activity. On the night of the 2nd, at 10.30 p.m. 2nd Lieutenant O. H. Staff, of the 18th Battalion, took out a patrol of eight men, leaving the trench at H1b 4.9 and moving down each side of the road. After completing his task 2nd Lieutenant Staff returned with his patrol but stated that he had seen Very lights go up on the left of the road. He declared his intention to go out again, in the hope of capturing some of the men who were sending up the lights. He departed again with Sergeant Steele and Private Morris. As they approached the point in question a machine gun opened fire on them and they were bombarded by a shower of hand grenades, one of them wounding Sergeant Steele. They were then pounced upon from behind by a party of Germans. In the following fight the trio became separated but Sergeant Steele was able to escape to the British lines. Some time later, he was followed by Private Morris, unwounded, who said that when he last saw 2nd Lieutenant Staff he was unwounded and fighting a party of about 12 Germans single-handed.

In the morning and afternoon of the 3rd, enemy artillery was very active, shelling the support trenches heavily. This, coupled with the experiences of the previous night, produced a tendency to 'over react'. As a result Private Gaunt was accidentally shot as he returned from an advanced post.

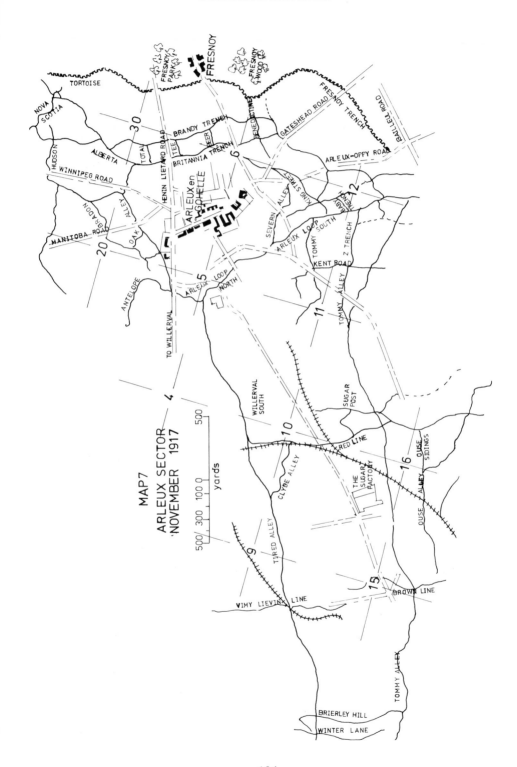

MAP 7
ARLEUX SECTOR
NOVEMBER 1917

No-man's land in front of Serre,1916. Imperial War Museum,*Neg. Q1910.*

CHAPTER 8: ARLEUX AND MERICOURT

O Jesus send me a wound today,
And I'll believe in bread and wine,
And get my bloody old sins washed white.
Siegfried Sassoon

On July 20th, the Brigade received orders to move to Neuville St. Vaast and thence to the line. The 16th Battalion reached their destination at 8.30 a.m. and rested until sundown in temporary billets before moving up to the trenches in front of Acheville. While the companies were moving off by platoons a few shells fell in the vicinity. One H.E. shell fell directly in front of 'D' Company who were just about to march off. 2nd Lieutenants Buchanan and Robb and four other ranks were killed, 41 others were wounded, one of whom later died.

The 16th Battalion occupied the front line with Battalion Headquarters in New Brunswick trench. The 15th Battalion were on the 16th's right, with the 11th East Yorks of the 92nd Brigade on their left. Their front line, with advanced post, which in fact were fortified shell holes, about 200 yards out, covered a frontage of about 1100 yards. The 18th Battalion moved into the trenches as battalion in support and worked as two 'double companies', 'A' and 'B' Company under Captain Key-Jones.

On the morning of the 22nd at 'stand down,' Corporal W. Ingram of 'A' Company, 16th Battalion, was found to be missing from one of the advanced posts. The circumstances pointed to him having been 'snatched' by an enemy patrol while making his way to a latrine. After this incident 'A' Company sent out patrols each night determined to catch an enemy straggler in order to even the score. One patrol, on the night of the 26th waited for 30 minutes outside the enemy wire, but without success. On the night of the 28th, which was exceedingly dark, Sergeant Nelson led out a patrol of six other ranks. 50 yards out from their own wire, they were surprised by an enemy patrol who opened fire on them at point blank range, from a shell hole concealed in long grass. The Sergeant fell, mortally wounded, whilst one other member of his party received lesser wounds.

The patrol was taken so unawares by the suddenness of the attack that with the exception of one bomb being thrown at the enemy, no retaliation was made. Two members of the patrol brought in the Sergeant's body, but Privates Claydon and Martin did not return and were posted missing.

Another misfortune befell the 16th Battalion that night when, at 1.00 a.m., the enemy shelled Quebec trench heavily. One shell fell outside 'C' Company Headquarters, killing a stretcher bearer of the 18th Battalion, mortally wounding 2nd Lieutenant O. L. Paus and wounding 2nd Lieutenant W. F. Caniey and three other ranks.

On the 29th, the 16th Battalion were relieved by the 11th East Lancashire Regiment, of the 94th Brigade and proceeded to the rear of the left Brigade L3 (Mericourt) Sector in Canada and 'Gertie Miller' trenches. The 18th Battalion occupied the front line on the right with the 18th Durhams on their left.

For the 16th, this dreary month closed with one bright spot. Each day, while in Brigade support, a party of 60 other ranks, together with a group of officers, proceeded after sundown to a point near Neuville St. Vaast to take hot baths, returning the following evening after sundown. George Morgan remembered this occasion well since it was his first opportunity to take a hot bath since he arrived in France. He had the dubious honour of sharing the same tub, in point of fact, a wine vat, with Company Sergeant Major Cussons.

On the night of August 1st, the 18th Battalion sent out patrols to examine the enemy wire. Patrol No. 1, under 2nd Lieutenant Burton with two N.C.O.'s and 19 other ranks with a Lewis gun, found the German wire to be three to four feet high and about seven yards deep with lots of loose wire, but no gaps. They returned to their own positions at 1.25 a.m. without incident. Patrol No. 2, under 2nd Lieutenant Kiddle with two N.C.O.'s and 20 other ranks with a Lewis gun, left their own lines at 9.40 a.m. at T17a 95 and moved north-east to the enemy entanglements and then moved south-east along the wire for about 280 yards. At this point they were challenged by a German sentry. Very lights were sent up and machine gun and rifle fire directed against them together with about 30 grenades thrown towards them. They withdrew without casualties after throwing grenades into the enemy trenches which were believed to cause casualties.

Both Battalions were relieved on the night of August 6th and rested for ten days, the 16th at Ottowa Camp and the 18th at Fraser Camp near Mont St. Eloy.

On August 16th they returned to the line, transported by train to Neuville St. Vaast and from there moving into the trenches. The 16th occupied the right sub-section in Totnes, Nova Scotia and Montreal trenches. 'A', 'B' and 'C' Companies were now commanded by Lieutenant E. Wilson, Captain G. W. Ashforth and Captain J. D. Ballantyne respectively.

The 18th had two companies in the railway embankment, known as Brown Line (see map 7) and two companies with Battalion Headquarters about A6c. The 16th spent their first day in the line generally cleaning up their trenches, and strengthening and deepening them. Patrols examined the wire, finding it deep and continuous. On the following day the Germans registered strong disapproval of their activities by bombarding the line with trench mortars and blowing in 15 yards of trench. The Battalion suffered four casualties from this fire, one of whom later died of his wounds.

On the night of August 19th, 540 gas projectors were discharged over Acheville. The attack was considered a success, the wind being favourable. Information obtained from a prisoner, captured later, indicated that his Regiment had suffered over 80 casualties from the gas with at least 20 dead. As dawn broke, the enemy retaliated with a *minen werfer* bombardment, 14 bombs bursting in and near the front line. One round burst in a bay, blowing to pieces a soldier who had just walked around the traverse and was actually saying *Good morning* to Sergeant Morgan who, with another soldier, was wounded by fragments. Suffering one large and two small wounds George Morgan, together with his comrade, was carried out amid calls of "What a lovely blighty". 2nd Lieutenant Metcalf was also wounded that day, hit by machine gun fire whilst visiting a forward post.

On the night of the 23rd patrols, each of one N.C.O. and ten other ranks, went out to examine the enemy wire on the Battalion's front. They found it to be deep and continuous.

On the following night. the 16th Battalion was relieved by the 13th Battalion the York and Lancaster Regiment and moved into the reserve line with 'A' and 'B' Companies in the Brickstacks. Battalion Headquarters was located in La Folie Wood. The troops were accommodated in dug outs in the old German line and although those in Vimy were continually shelled, everyone was said to be comfortable. Bath houses had now been erected for the use of the troops, in the Brickfields and in Vimy East, no doubt making a considerable contribution to the comfort of the accommodation. They were to remain in the reserve line engaged in fatigues, deepening and widening Teddie Gerade trench and carrying mining cases and gun pit frames to Hudson trench until the night of the 4th September when they were relieved by the 4th Canadian Mounted Rifles and moved to Kitchener Camp, north of Roclincourt.

From 2.00 a.m. to 3.00 a.m. on the 30th August, the enemy heavily shelled the 18th Battalion's Headquarters in the Quarry, their front line in Totnes trench and their close support and support positions in Quebec and New Brunswick trenches, more especially on the front line where this trench cut the Quarries Road. From 9.00 a.m. to 12 noon and from 2.00 p.m.

until nearly 7.00 p.m., with very isolated intervals, the Battalion Headquarters was shelled severely, about 1,000 shells of all calibres falling in and around the Quarry. So indiscriminate and careless was the nature of this shelling against the various lines of trenches that it hardly gave the idea of registration or barrage firing. Lieutenant-Colonel Carter reached the conclusion that the enemy was trying to hide his registration and practise barrage firing by excessive shelling in the guise of a destructive shoot against the Colonel's Headquarters, and that the enemy's intention was to raid his positions.

The front line, Totnes trench, was manned by 100 men. Another 80 men were in close support in Quebec trench whilst the strength of the Company of the 15th Battalion in New Brunswick was roughly 70 men. On studying the map, Lieutenant-Colonel Carter realised that if the enemy were to make an accurate entry into some definite point in the front line, he would need some obvious mark to guide him, in the dark, across a No-man's-land of some 600 to 800 yards width. As most of the shelling had been on the left and the fact that the Quarries Road would make the only definite guide for the enemy to a definite point, he concluded that the most probable point of attack would be the junction of Totnes trench and Quarries Road and its vicinity. Lieutenant-Colonel Carter therefore issued the following instructions:

(1) The following orders were sent to companies at 1 p.m., the letter being addressed to 'C' Company (left flank) and copies sent to other companies: "The shelling today looks as if the Bosche may be thinking of a raid on your front. With this in view do no wiring tonight, nor will the other companies. If you think it advisable you can put a small listening patrol just in front of your wire and possibly a post to your left rear in that old disused trench, south of the Quarries Road and behind your front line, in case he tries to get in behind you.

Warn your men, and 'D' Company Commander will lend you half his strength, whom you can put on your left in Quebec, and these with any of 'A' or 'B' Companies left in the line can be used for counter attacking. The working party of 20 in 12th Avenue belonging to Hilt [15th Battalion the West

Yorkshire Regiment] will in case of trouble, come automatically under your orders and I will write to them to this effect.

Directly you counter attack, send a runner over the top to Hilt's Company in New Brunswick and tell them to come up and reinforce you in Quebec. Send a wire to me when you have counter attacked too. I will send the remainder of Hilt to you in case they have not received your message. This is only in case a raid takes place. If of course the raid is on 'A' or 'B' Company's front, 'A' or 'B' Company will take charge of the counter attack with the oddments of 'A', 'B', 'C' Companies and half 'D' Company.

No stores will be drawn tonight and half 'D' Company will do all the ration carrying for tonight. Be careful of water today in case the well is blown in."

(2)   The following orders have been given to Hilt Company attached to me. "The shelling today rather points to the possibility of a raid on our left front.

In this case we have to counter attack, you will, if you receive orders from either me or one of the Company Commanders in Quebec move across over the lid and take up the defence of Quebec. Explain this to your men, and that they are only on the defensive, and that my Battalion will be in front of them. Also, do not move your bombing post just north of junction of Quarries Road and New Brunswick trench.

Your working party in 12th Avenue will, in case of trouble, report to officer commanding 'C' Company in Quebec."

Lieutenant-Colonel
Commanding Officer Haze

A standing patrol was positioned between the Battalion's left (point A on map 8) and the 18th Durham Light Infantry to cover the gap which existed there.

The night of the 31st was quiet until 2.45 a.m. when the enemy put down a heavy barrage of 5.9's, 4.2's, 4.1's and 77mm shells on the front line, close support and support trenches.

Lieutenant-Colonel Carter went to the top of the Quarry and watched the barrage develop.

Between 2.45 a.m. and 3.00 a.m. the Lewis gun post on the left flank spotted a party of about 30 Germans approaching the wire in single file. At the same time No. 3 post of the left company observed a similar party, carrying a machine gun, approaching. Immediately both posts opened rapid fire. In answer to the sentries shouts of

"Stand to! They're comin' ower"

men leapt to the parapet and, with rifles and Lewis guns, poured a fire into the enemy parties, the companies on the right firing half left. Many enemy were seen to drop. During all this time the enemy artillery barrage continued to rain down on the pararet, killing 2nd Lieutenant R. G. Dalton and one other rank and wounding eight other ranks.

Captain W. Peace

Shortly after the fight began, a wounded man came back into the support trench and told Captain Whittaker who commanded 'A' Company that he thought the enemy had entered the line on the left. Captain Whittaker immediately signalled by telephone 'S.O.S.L3' and ordered the officer-in-charge of the light trench mortar battery to "Open fire."

Following the orders previously received, Captain Peace, Commanding 'C' Company, together with the half of 'D' Company attached to him, counter attacked 'Over the lid' to Totnes trench. The leading party jumped into an empty bay and began working up the trench whilst the men following worked from outside the trench. At the same time as the counter attack moved off, the 15th West Yorks Company moved forward to take up the defence of Quebec trench (marked E on the map).

As soon as this was done Lieutenant-Colonel Carter sent a message to the front line companies instructing them that as soon as the front line was clear they were to push out strong patrols to search for German dead and wounded and that, if possible, all men were to be back in their original positions by dawn. In point of fact the enemy had not entered the front line and had not penetrated beyond the wire. There was some delay in sending out patrols due to difficulties in stopping the trench mortar barrage, which had been deadly accurate and caused a great deal of damage. Many of the enemy killed or wounded by Lewis gun and rifle fire were blown to bits where they lay. Decimated remains of many German corpses were found in front of the wire. Only one wounded German, with both his legs broken, was found and brought in, together with the body of an officer wearing the ribbon of the Iron Cross and other orders. Both men belonged to the 54th Infantry Regiment. Although the remains of some six to ten dead Germans were found, these were in such a decimated state that identification was impossible and collection for burial considered "not worthwhile." The booty recovered by the search parties included a light machine gun, in good condition and clean, a wooden encased bangalore torpedo, a Very pistol and three rifles.

Four snipers, in camouflage suits, crawled out into No-man's-land and searched the ground for any wounded or dead. Each carried a card, written in German, explaining to anyone they found that they were in good hands and if they remained quiet they would be brought in after dark. These men returned at 3.30 p.m. without finding anyone.

The following memorandums, congratulating the Battalion in their repulse of the raid, were later received from Brigadier-General J. D. Ingles and Brigadier-General Ian Stewart:

C. C. HAZE

I congratulate you on the thoroughness and excellence of your arrangements in repelling the raid attempted by the enemy against your lines on the morning of the 31st and on your success which you thoroughly deserved.

I also wish to express my great appreciation of the splendid behaviour and prompt action of the Officers, N.C.O.'s and men of your Battalion and the determined manner in which they carried out your orders.

J. D. Ingles, Brigadier-General

31st August 1917   Commanding 93rd Infantry Brigade

31st Division

The Corps Commander has read with interest the report on the attempted raid of the 31st August, and requests that you will convey his congratulations to the C.O. 18th West Yorks Regiment, and the troops under his command on the accurate appreciation of the enemy's intentions, and adequate steps taken to frustrate them and the confidence and promptitude displayed in meeting the attack.

XIII Corps.   Signed: Ian Stewart

4th September 1917   Brigadier-General, General Staff

On the 4th September, the 18th Battalion mounted two daylight patrols. Here are their official reports:

18th West Yorks Regiment
DAYLIGHT PATROL REPORT
4th September, 1917

Two observers in camouflaged suits left our left company front at 4.35 a.m., crossed the Quarries Road and the Miericourt Road and proceeded to about T11a 25.

At 5.45 a.m., they saw a party of 12 men leave the sandbag structure at T11a 55 (approx.) previously reported and proceeded to their front line. 100 yards to left of sandbag structure is an S-shaped SAP, the head of which is apparently a shell hole. At 6.30 a.m. six enemy with a M.G. left this SAP for their front line. In the SAP head is a T.M.[trench mortar] about 12 inches long pointing in the direction of the battalion on our left.

The White House is about 100 yards behind enemy line, in a direct line with the sandbag structure. Behind and to the right of White House there is a house built at right angles, and in the end of this, about 15 feet from the ground is a square sandbagged hole, probably a M.G. emplacement or an O.P. In front of White House, quite close, is a dump of barbed wire, trench elements and iron stakes.

At 1.00 p.m., about 14 stretchers were taken to the cemetery. Could not be seen whether they contained dead or wounded.

At 1.30 p.m., observers saw what was apparently a long round periscope in enemy front line to the right of communication trench leading to the White House. They thought they might be seen, so fired simultaneously and smashed it.

3.00 p.m. Four Germans were seen to move along front line and climb over portion of trench which had been blown in. On their backs were strapped metal objects 2 feet by 1 foot 6 inches, with a tube on the top. Probably Vermosel sprayers.

At 5.30 pm observers saw working party of 100 men carrying shovels and rifles going past the White House, to the rear of enemy lines.

At 6.00 p.m, on the left edge of the Quarries Road, about T11a 55.15, there are three dead Germans, recently killed, probably some of the raiding party of 31.8.17. They could not get close enough to examine them because the road at this point is in full view of the enemy.

The enemy has put out a lot of wire since the last patrol, on 30.8.17. The fork roads at T11a 61 are heavily wired.

11.30 a.m. Our artillery were firing on the enemy line in rear of the sandbag structure. Observers think enemy had a number of casualties, for whistles were constantly being blown. They think this was a signal for stretcher bearers. They report that artillery which was firing on the enemy front line to the right of Quarries Road was making accurate shooting, shells were falling in the trench and on the parapet.

When the enemy fired at our aircraft, they noticed there were quite a number of machine guns between SAP referred to before, and the Quarries Road. Eight machine guns were plainly seen. Observers returned to our lines at 8.30 p.m.

DAYLIGHT PATROL 3rd September, 1917

Patrol of two other ranks left our lines at 4.30 a.m. At 5.30 a.m. patrol saw enemy moving back from front line to support line independently. About 90 O. R. were seen. This confirms previous report and would seem to indicate that the enemy vacates his front line during the day. If our artillery shelled between 5.00 a.m. and 6.00 a.m. each morning they would be certain of causing casualties. Communication trench running into Mericourt-Acheville Road, seems to be a popular route. M.G.'s fired on our planes from front and support lines. Enemy guns, 4.2's, were observed to be firing from behind hedges at T18d 57. There seem to be several batteries firing from this part of Acheville.

The 18th Battalion were relieved from the line on the night of the 5th September, and moved back to Neuville St. Vaast where they later entrained for Bray. Both battalions now enjoyed a brief respite from the front line in their respective camps. Their time was spent in resting or training, although the 16th Battalion detached one company, first 'C' and later 'A', on a working detail in Long Wood.

On September 19th, both battalions returned to trench duty, the 16th relieving the 11th East Yorkshire Regiment in the L2 sub-section of the Arleux Sector, the 15th West Yorkshire Regiment being on their right and the 14th York and Lancaster Regiment, 94th Brigade, being the battalion on their left. The relief was completed in daylight via Tired Alley. The 18th Battalion moved into the support positions known as Red Line (see map 7) relieving the 10th East Yorkshire Regiment.

On the 25th the 18th Battalion moved into the front line, relieving the 15th West Yorkshire Regiment, in the right battalion position, whilst the 16th were relieved by the 18th Durham Light Infantry and took over that Battalion's position in the left support sector, with 'A' Company in the Arleux Loop and 'B', 'C' and 'D' Companies in Red Line. The War Diary records that during the preceding tour in the front line, the Battalion suffered only two casualties, both wounded although one seriously, and one case of suspected shell shock. On October 1st, the 16th was relieved by the 12th East Yorkshire

Regiment and moved to Bray. The 18th was relieved by the 10th East Yorkshire Regiment and occupied the support line for five-days. Then they too moved to Bray, having been relieved from support by the 13th East Yorkshire Regiment. There followed for both battalions a spell of eight days of rest, specialist training with Lewis guns, bangolore torpedoes and practice firing on the Bray range. On the 13th, both battalions were moved back into the line, the 18th occupying the support trenches.

On the 16th October at 5.10 a.m., the enemy brought down an extra heavy bombardment on the positions occupied by the 16th Battalion, wounding Lieutenant J. L. Stanley, D.S.O., and three other ranks, one from 'C' Company the others from 'D' Company. The bombardment also extended to the battalions on their left and right flanks, the 14th York and Lancaster Regiment and the 15th West Yorks respectively. Lieutenant-Colonel A. C. Croydon, M.C., seeing this to be no ordinary affair called for artillery retaliation, soon after which the York and Lancaster Battalion sent up S.O.S. rockets. The artillery retaliation which resulted probably stopped the enemy mounting a raid. He did mount a raid against the York and Lancaster Regiment, but his efforts proved unsuccessful. Half the enemy troops never reached the British wire, having been caught in the S.O.S. barrage. One prisoner was taken by the York and Lancaster's who subsequently counted 27 dead in their wire. At 10.00 a.m. a Red Cross flag was waved from the German second line, the enemy presumably wishing to search for and bring in wounded, but as no one appeared and enemy shelling continued, no action was taken in response to this gesture.

After the raid, as it was thought that a number of the enemy might be laying out in No-man's-land awaiting an opportunity to 'crawl in' after dark Sergeant G. Meadows of 'C' Company, 16th Battalion, asked permission to go out, dressed in a camouflaged suit, and see if he could spot any of the enemy and if so, "account for them." Permission was granted and he crawled out, with one other rank following in the rear to give support and assistance. After they had crawled about 150 yards, they saw two enemy soldiers laying a telephone wire. Sergeant Meadows fired at and killed the leading man. The other man immediately took cover but presently reappeared, whereupon the Sergeant fired again killing this man also. A third man then appeared but although the Sergeant fired at him, he was successful in getting away. After this Sergeant Meadows and his companion remained in No-man's land for some considerable time but, observing no other enemy, they then returned to their own lines. Sergeant Meadows was later awarded a Military Medal.

On the night of 19th October, the 18th Battalion relieved the 15th West Yorks in the front line, whilst the 16th Battalion were relieved by the 18th Durhams and moved into left support with three companies in Red Line and one company in Arleux Loop South.

Both battalions remained in these positions until the 25th October when they were relieved from the line, the 16th Battalion moving to Durham and Lancaster camps whilst the 18th Battalion moved to Bray. This was followed by almost two weeks rest and training before both battalions returned to trench duty. This pattern of movement was to continue for the next three months.

The winter of 1917-1918 was one of the hardest on record. Extremely cold weather froze the ground to the hardness of iron. The battle front was covered by a carpet of snow. Operations were impeded on both sides and although the front was officially described as 'quiet', life in the trenches was exceedingly difficult. Nevertheless, both battalions maintained a policy of aggressive patrolling in No-man's land.

Examples of these activities recorded in the 18th Battalion's diary are:

23rd October - Daylight patrol from 'C' Company commenced detailed reconnaissance of enemy wire.

25th October - Daylight patrol located three enemy machine guns in a shell hole at B12b 80.05.

10th November - Daylight patrol went out at 6.30 a.m. returning at 11.00 a.m. after reconnoitring enemy defences. Three hostile machine guns located. Second daylight patrol examined enemy wire. Third daylight patrol worked south-east along Oppy-Arleux Road as far as Willows. Reported light trench mortar firing from SAP in front of enemy line behind Willows.

14th November - Patrol of five men led by Corporal Barker took up a position in No-man's-land under cover of mist. At about 7.15 a.m., a sentry was seen with his head and shoulders above parapet of enemy SAP. Corporal Barker fired at this man who threw up his hands and disappeared groaning.

An interesting example of ground / air liaison occurred on November 15th, when three patrols, each of two other ranks crawled out into No-man's- land and marked the position of enemy machine guns firing at British aeroplanes which, by arrangement, flew low overhead to draw fire from the enemy's guns.

On January 4th, news was received that Temporary Major (Acting Lieutenant-Colonel) A. C. Croydon was promoted to the rank of Temporary Lieutenant-Colonel. Also an extract from the London Gazette, War Office, dated 18th December, 1917 was published in Battalion Orders:

> Mentioned in Despatches 7th November, 1917
> Lieutenant-Colonel A. C. Croydon,M.C.
> Lieutenant J. L. Stanley, D.S.O.
> Lieutenant J. M. Barrow
> Lieutenant D. T. King
> Lance Corporal W. Francis

The hard winter weather was followed by heavy rain and a rapid thaw. Conditions became very bad, subsidences taking place and the bottom of the trenches becoming, in places, two or three feet deep in thick adhesive mud. Communication trenches became impassable and movement was only possible 'over the top'. Consequently during the hours of daylight the advanced posts were completely isolated. However, Mother Nature was not selective, the conditions in the German line being equally abhorrent. The 18th Battalion War Diaries record that "visibility was very bad and there was exceedingly little activity on either side." The 16th Battalion, however, reported heavy shelling around the Tunnel Headquarters and some artillery fire directed at the Sucrerie and Willerval.

Daylight patrol leaving snow-covered front line trench, Arleux Sector, 1917. *Imperial War Museum, Negative Q 10624.*

On the night of the 19th the 18th Battalion were relieved from the front line by the 18th Durham Light Infantry and moved to Ecurie Wood. This completed their last tour in the front line. The 16th, on the night of the 23rd, moved into close support in Red Line, with 'D' Company in Arleux Loop North. Until their relief from these positions on the 27th, when they moved to billets in Ecoivres every available man was employed in making the trenches passable, particularly Arleux Loop and Tired Alley.

At Ecoivres, after the usual cleaning up and kit inspections, the companies were reorganized into three platoons per company.

On January 31st, orders were received by the 18th to "disband the battalion." The 16th, however, were to complete one more tour of trench duty. On February 5th they relieved the 11th East Yorkshire Regiment in the Arleux Sub-Sector. The companies were distributed as follows:

'A' and 'B' Companies under Captain Battishill, M.C., in Arleux Post; 'C' Company under Captain L. L. de Souza in Oak Post; 'D' Company under Captain A. H. Evans in Tommy Post.

Arleux Loop had been heavily bombarded by howitzers, during the morning prior to be relief and about 50 yards of trench had been blown in. Baron trench was also subjected to heavy machine gun fire during the day. The 6th was marked by the heavy artillery bombardment of the German lines owing to the

119

expected relief of the 240th Division by the 5th Bavarian Regiment. The Battalion participated with machine gun, Lewis gun and trench mortar fire.

During the next few days, a great deal of work was done in clearing the mud from Arleux Loop and repairing the damage to Baron trench. These activities were interrupted on the night of the 8th when the enemy put down a heavy barrage on the right divisional sector, occupied by the 62nd Division. This was followed by a raid, which was repulsed, two of the enemy and two British soldiers being killed.

Men resting in trench shelters, Arleux Sector, 1917. *Imperial War Museum, Negative C 01285.*

On the 11th February 1918 the Battalion was relieved from the front line for the last time, by the 18th Durham Light Infantry, and moved to Fraser Camp. On the following day they marched to Maroeuil where they were billeted in the town. On the 13th, Company Sergeant Major G. Cussons ceased to perform the duties of acting Regimental Sergeant Major, being posted to the 15th Battalion West Yorkshire Regiment. Captain L. H. Croxford and Lieutenant D. T. King of 'A' Company, together with 2nd Lieutenant J. Luke of 'D' Company were also 'cross posted' to the 15th Battalion, as were 192 other ranks.

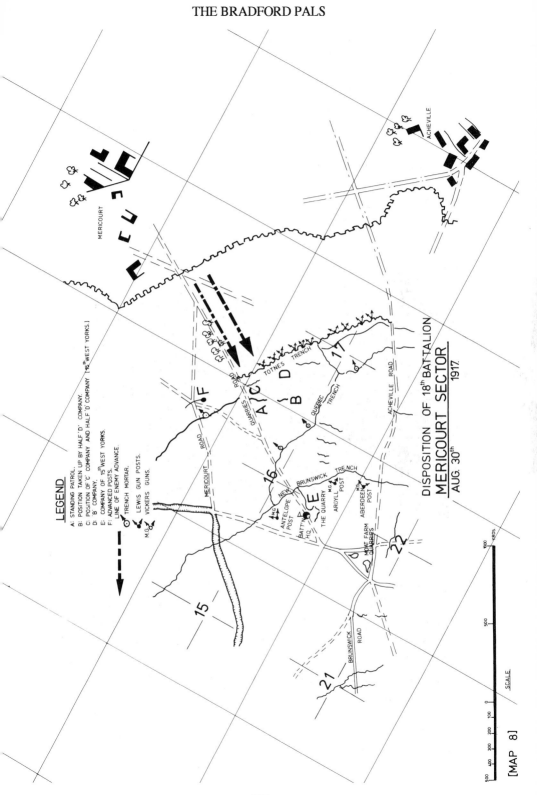

LEGEND

A: STANDING PATROL.
B: POSITION TAKEN UP BY HALF 'D' COMPANY.
C: POSITION OF 'C' COMPANY AND HALF 'D' COMPANY [16th WEST YORKS.]
D: 'B' COMPANY.
E: COMPANY OF 15th WEST YORKS.
F: ADVANCED POSTS.
LINE OF ENEMY ADVANCE.
TRENCH MORTAR.
LEWIS GUN POSTS.
M.G.O. VICKERS GUNS.

DISPOSITION OF 18th BATTALION
MERICOURT SECTOR
AUG. 30th 1917.

[MAP 8]

SCALE

121

The Prince of Wales inspects Old Comrades in Bradford in the Twenties.

Survivors of the Pals battalions at Bradford Cenotaph, July 1st, 1977.
Bradford Telegraph and Argus.

Aftermath

Have you forgotten yet? ...
For the world's events have rumbled on since those gagged
days,
Like traffic checked while at the crossing of city-ways:
And the haunted gap in your mind has filled with thoughts that
flow
Like clouds in the lit heaven of life; and you're a man reprieved
to go,
Taking your peaceful share of time, with joy to spare.
But the past is just the same - and War's a bloody game ...
Have you forgotten yet? ...
Look down, and swear by the slain of the War that you'll never
forget.

Do you remember the dark months you held the sector at
Mametz -
The nights you watched and wired and dug and piled sandbags
on parapets?
Do you remember the rats; and the stench
Of corpses rotting in front of the front line trench -
And dawn coming, dirty-white, and chill with a hopeless rain?
Do you ever stop and ask, "Is it all going to happen again?"

Do you remember that hour of din before the attack -
And the anger, the blind compassion that seized and shook you
then
As you peered at the doomed and haggard faces of your men?
Do you remember the stretcher cases lurching back
With dying eyes and lolling heads - those ashen-grey
Masks of the lads who once were keen and kind and gay?

Have you forgotten yet? ...
Look up, and swear by the green of the spring that you'll never
forget.

Siegfried Sassoon. March, 1919.

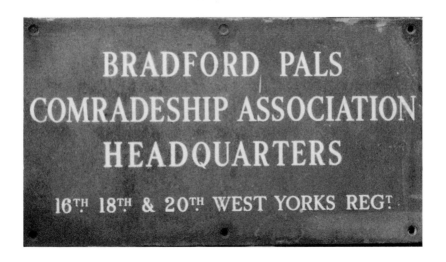

CHAPTER 9: AND IN THE END

On February 15th, 1918, the 16th Battalion marched to Mont St. Eloi Station and entrained for Pernes. From there they marched to Sachin, about two miles to the east, where they were billeted under XIII Corps instructions.The last entry in the battalion's War Diary reads:

"February 28th - The total strength of the Battalion (583 other ranks) and the undermentioned officers are posted to the 3rd Entrenching Battalion and proceed to join."

Officers on the Battalion strength at that time were:

Headquarters

Lieutenant-Colonel A. C. Croydon, M.C., D.C.M.,
Commanding
Acting Major W. D. Coles
Captain and Adjutant J. J. G. Greenwood
Captain A. J. Brightwell
Captain G. A. McK Morant, M.C.
Lieutenant J. M. Barrow
2nd Lieutenant T. S. Campbell

'A' Company
Captain P. H. Battishill, M.C.
Captain L. H. Croxford
Lieut E. Wilson
2nd Lieut J. R. Brown
2nd Lieut F. de B. Price
2nd Lieut L. Crabtree
2nd Lieut S. S. L. Jackson
2nd Lieut K. T. Makin

'B' Company
Captain H. S. Nesbitt
2nd Lieut W. Barrie
2nd Lieut J. F. Farrar
2nd Lieut J. P. Lawson
2nd Lieut L. Parsey, D.C.M.
2nd Lt. A .L. Pearson,DCM.

'C' Company
Captain J. D. Ballantyne
Captain L. L. de Souza
Lieutenant A. Dickes
2nd Lieut G. A. Brown
2nd Lieut A. J. Comerford
2nd Lieut J. J. Walton
2nd Lieut R. Ward
2nd Lieut A. B. P. Wood

'D' Company
Captain H.Evans
Captain E. Murgatroyd, D.C.M.
Lieut O. V. L. Hough
Lieut J. L.Richard
2nd Lieutt H. J. Clements
2nd Lieut J. P. Feather
2nd Lieut D. G. Garbutt
2nd Lt. R. W. Jackson, D.C.M.
2nd Lieut E. Jowett
2nd Lieut G.L. Lyall
2nd Lieut J. W. Marsden

Attached to Battalion
Captain C. Roche, M.C., R.A.M.C. (Medical Officer)
Captain J. Calderbank (Church of England Chaplain)

The 18th Battalion, having spent four days as Brigade support in the Arleux Sector, moved to Bray camp. On February 1st, all officers and other ranks assembled in the camp Church Army hut where Lieutenant-Colonel Carter explained the reasons for disbanding the Battalion and expressed his appreciation of the manner in which all ranks had worked under him.

On the days which followed, drafts began to leave the Battalion, although it was a great consolation to all that the drafts were to other battalions in the Regiment. Officers on the strength at that time were:

Lieutenant-Colonel H. F. G. Carter, M.C., Commanding
Captain H. L. Dalley, M.C., Adjutant
Captain M. Clough
Captain F. W. Whittacker
Captain L. H. Bakes
Major A. W. Robinson
Lieutenant J. L. Wood
Lieutenant F. R. Kennington
Lieutenant and Q/ M B. Hammond
Lieutenant J. R. King
Lieutenant F. D. Dams
Lieutenant E. Williams
Lieutenant A. Cockenham
Lieutenant E. A. Ramsden

2nd Lieut A. Atkinson

2nd Lieut F. G. Baker

2nd Lieut T. E. Dickenson

2nd Lieut C. H. Duckworth

2nd Lieut H. Gill

2nd Lieut J. Gray

2nd Lieutenant J. D. Hollis

2nd Lieutenant W. R. Horner

2nd Lieutenant F. H. Hoyle

2nd Lieut C. F. Kiddle

2nd Lieut G. R. Lorel

2nd Lieut A. S. Penn

2nd Lieut H. Salmons

2nd Lieut P. H. Scott

2nd Lieut E. Smith

2nd Lieut G. W. Smith

2nd Lieut C. A. F. Thornton

2nd Lieut J. Whithead

2nd Lieut J. Whithead

2nd Lieut R. B. Wright

On February 11th, a farewell message from the Brigadier, was received:

"The Brigade Commander feels sure that Brigadier-General J. D. Ingles, D.S.O., who is now on leave would wish to express to Lieutenant Colonel H. F. G. Carter, M.C., and Lieutenant Colonel A. C. Croydon, M.C., and all ranks of the 16th and 18th Battalions, West Yorkshire Regiment his deep sense of regret at parting from them as units of the 93rd Brigade. Both these battalions have served in the 93rd Brigade since its formation in May 1915, and have loyally and devotedly upheld the splendid traditions of their Regiment, and have by their good work and efficiency, largely contributed to the high reputation of the Brigade.

The severance of these battalions from the Brigade is necessary in the interests of the whole army, but that does not lessen the deep regret felt throughout all the remaining ranks of the Brigade.

In times of hardship and danger, the 16th and 18th Battalions of the West Yorkshire Regiment have proved themselves brave, cheerful soldiers and good comrades.

To all ranks of these battalions, the best wishes of the Brigade are tendered for their success and welfare in the future, and they will never be forgotten."

On February 15th, Lieutenant-Colonel Carter together with Major A. W. Robinson, Captain L. H. Bakes, Lieutenant J. L. Wood, Lieutenant B. Hammond, Lieutenant F. R. Kennington, 2nd Lieutenant G. W. Smith and 2nd Lieutenant F. H. Hoyle together with 42 other ranks proceeded by rail to the XIII Corps reinforcement camp at Pernes. The last entry in the Diary, referring to this posting, reads:

"This reduced the strength of the battalion in the field to NIL".

So ends the story of the *Bradford Pals*. No longer the keen boisterous battalions of volunteers who had marched from Bradford three and a half years previously and been thrice decimated in battle, but men who never lost faith for all that.

After the war the survivors formed the "Bradford Pals Old Comrades' Association" with its headquarters at: 'Claremont, 'Morley Street, Bradford. This Association was active until March 1979.

The King's Colours of both battalions now hang in Bradford Cathedral, near the side door. However, one cannot fail to comment on the fact that, when peace came, the City which had raised them did not put up a memorial, nor a plaque to those *Pals* who did not return, until July 1979.

It is fashionable now to write of these men as 'brainwashed by the system;' 'carried away by misguided enthusiasm;' 'men who did not know what they were fighting for.' Anyone who has had the fortune, indeed the honour, to meet these men, knows this not to be so. In 1976 after spending an evening in the Blighty Club with a group of *Old Pals*, which included George Morgan,

Frank Burn and Frank Hartley, listening to their experiences on the Somme and the other battlefields of the First World War, the author expressed the view that what seemed so incredible was the impression that, if asked to do the same again, they would. Almost as one voice these old comrades replied: "Yes, we would!"

Perhaps the words of Winston Churchill in his book *World crisis* would make a fitting farewell to these battalions:

If only Generals had not been content to fight machine gun bullets with the breasts of gallant men, and to think that that was waging war.

George Taylor at Serre Cemetery in 1974 photographed by Stan Barraclough. Field Marshal Haig: *I consider the machine gun to be a greatly over-rated weapon.*

APPENDIX 1: Officers died in the Great war, 1914-19: extract of entries for the 16th and 18th battalions.

16th BATTALION:

Armitage, Geoffrey Ambler, Capt. (Tp.), k. in a., 27/2/17.
Blagbrough, George Stanley, Major (Tp.), k. in a., 11/12/16, (att. from East Yorks. Regiment).
Clough, Alan, Temp. Capt., k. in a., 1/7/16.
Greville, David Onslow, 2/Lt., k. in a., 3/5/17.
Hyde, Charles Stuart, T/2/Lt., k. in a., 1/7/16.
Jackson, Robert William, M.C., 2/Lt., k. in a., 23/10/18 (att. from 1st Bn.).
Knight, Walter Foster, T/Lt., k. in a., 27/2/17 (att. from 14th Bn.)
Laxton, Reginald Earl,, T/2/Lt., k. in a., 10/6/16.
Long, Bernard Wilfrid, T/2/Lt., k. in a., 16/8/17.
Morant, Gerald Alexander Mackay, M.C., T/Capt., k. in a., 15/4/18 (att. 2/5th Bn).
Newlands, Sidney Barron, T/2/Lt., k. in a., 1/7/16.
Paus, Oscar Lionel, T/2/Lt., d. of w., 29/7/17.
Platnauer, Leonard Maurice, 2/Lt., d. of w., 3/5/17.
Pringle, Robert William Hey, T/Capt., k. in a., 1/7/16.
Ransome, Cecil Talbot, T/Lt., k. in a., 1/7/16.
Robb, John, 2/Lt., (Tp.) k. in a., 21/7/17.
Robinson, John Holdsworth, 2/Lt., k. in a., 1/7/16.
Russell, Henry, Capt., (Tp.) d. of w., 10/6/16.
Smith, Donald, Temp. Capt., k. in a., 1/7/16.
Stead, Ralph, 2/Lt. (Tp.) k. in a., 1/7/16.
Sutcliffe, Robert, 2/Lt., d. of w., 5/7/16.
Symonds, Frank James, Temp. 2/lt., k. in a., 1/7/16.
Tweedale, Eric, 2/Lt., (Tp.), K. in a., 1/7/16 (att. from 13th Bn.).
Webster, Michael Harold, Lt. (Tp.), k. in a., 1/7/16 (att. from 13th Bn.).

18th BATTALION:

Akam, James Rhodes, Lt., k. in a., 1/7/16.
Baker, Frederick Gerald, 2/Lt., (Tp.), k. in a., 17/4/18.
Clough, Morris, Capt., k. in a., 25/4/18.
Colley, Harold, 2/Lt., k. in a., 1/7/16.
Cross, Ronald Sidney, Capt., (Tp.) k. in a., 27/7/16.
Dalton, Richard Gregory, T/2/Lt., k. in a., 31/8/17.
De Lacy, John Matthew, 2/Lt., k. in a., 23/9/17 (and R.F.C., 57 Sqn.).
Derwent, Robert Ivor, 2/Lt. k. in a., 1/7/16.
Duckitt, Charles Stanley, T/Capt., k. in a., 3/5/17.
Foizey, Harold Egbert, Lt. (Tp.), K. in a., 1/7/16.
Gill, Daniel, T/2/Lt., k. in a., 24/10/16.
Gray, John, 2/Lt., died, 26/11/18.
Holt, Wifrid, 2/Lt., k. in a.,3/5/17.
Hummel, Raymond, T/2/Lt., k. in a., 19/5/16.
Humphries, Walter Rawleigh, 2/Lt. (Tp.) k. in a., 27/7/16.
Jones, Robert Henry, T/2/Lt., k. in a., 29/6/16 (att. from 13th Bn.).
Keevil, Cecil Horace Case, T/Capt., killed, 13/6/17 (and R.F.C.).
Kennard, Maurice Nicholl, T/Lt.-Col., k. in a., 1/7/16.
King, John Rose, M.C., Lt. (Tp.), k. in a., 22/4/18 (att. 10th Bn.).
Mansfield, Harold Lawrie, 2/Lt., d. of w., 3/5/17.
Moulson, Samuel, T/2/Lt., k. in a., 4/9/18.
Nowell, Francis Percival, T/2/Lt., d. of w., 2/7/16.
Robinson, Frank Victor, Lt. (Tp.), k. in a., 3/5/17.
Sleigh, William Ward, Lt., (Tp.), k. in a., 25/2/17.
Smith, John Taylor, Temp. 2/Lt., d. of w., 29/3/18 (att. 2nd Bn.).
Tooke, Bernard, Temp. Capt., k. in a., 3/5/17.
Walton, Francis John George, 2/Lt., (Tp.), k. in a., 1/7/16.
Warner, William James, 2/Lt., k. in a., 3/5/17.
Watson, Frank, Lt., k. in a., 1/7/16 (att. 03 T.M.B.).
Williams, Eric, Lt., k. in a., 27/3/18, (att. 2nd Bn.).
Worsnop, John William, 2/Lt., k. in a., 30/6/16.

Facsimile of the pages relating to the 16th and 18th battalions.
British Crown Copyright, 1991 MoD, reproduced with the
permission of the Controller of HMSO.

APPENDIX 2: Soldiers died in the Great War, 1914-19: Facsimile of the pages relating to the 16th and 18th battalions.

British Crown Copyright, 1991 MoD, reproduced with the permission of the Controller of HMSO.

Explanation of abbreviations:

"b." - "born."
"e." - "enlisted."
"d." - "died."
"d. of w." - "died of wound."
"k. in a." - "killed in action."
"F. & F." - "France & Flanders
(including Italy).

16th Battalion.

Abrey, Charles Frederick, b. West Ham, London, e. Stratford, 9440, Pte., 27/2/17.

Ackroyd, George, b. Matlock, Derbyshire, e. Matlock, 19281, Pte, d. of w., F. & F., 1/3/17.

Ackroyd, Willie, b. Bradford, e. Bradford, Yorks, 16/682, Pte., k. in a., F. & F., 27/7/16.

Airton, George Beecroft, b. Yeadon, Yorks, e. Bradford, Yorks, 16/1343, Sgt., k. in a., F. & F., 1/7/16.

Aked, Clement, b. Cleckheaton, Yorks, e. Bradford, Yorks (Eccleshill, Bradford), 16/858, Pte., k. in a., F. & F., 1/7/16.

Alcock, William, b. Bradford, e. Bradford, Yorks, 33530, Pte., k. in a., F. & F., 3/5/17.

Alderson, Henry, b. Leeds, e. North Shields (North Shields), 19821, Pte., d. of w., F. & F., 1/3/17.

Ambler, Victor, b. Eccleshill, Bradford, Yorks, e. Bradford, 16/739, Sgt., k. in a., F. & F., 1/7/16.

Anderson, George, b. Ripon, e. Ripon, Yorks, 25060, Pte., d. of w., F. & F., 11/9/17.

Arkley, John, b. Sunderland, e. Sunderland, 4/8145, L/Cpl., k. in a., F. & F., 3/5/17.

Arnold, Edmund Gilyard, b. Eccleshill, Bradford, Yorks, e. Bradford, 16/1264, Pte., k. in a., F. & F., 1/7/16.

Arundel, Percy, b. Leeds, e. Leeds, 37527, Pte., d. of w., F. & F., 28/8/17.

Arthington, Ernest Harry, b. Bradford, e. Bradford, Yorks, 16/1141, Pte., k. in a., F. & F., 1/7/16.

Aveyard, John Hodgson, b. Bradford, e. Bradford, Yorks, 16/1140, k. in a., F. & F., 1/7/16.

Backhouse, Sidney, e. Wetherby, Yorks, 31999, Pte., k. in a., F. & F., 13/11/16.

Baldock, Claude Henry, b. Nottingham, e. Nottingham, 41713, Pte., k. in a., F. & F., 3/5/17., formerly 49311, K.O.Y.L.I.

Balme, Benjamin, b. Clayton, Bradford, Yorks, e. Bradford, 16/736, Pte., k. in a., F. & F., 1/7/16.

Bannister, William, b. Bradford, e. Bradford, Yorks, 16/438, Pte., k. in a., F. & F., 24/4/16.

Barker, Alfred, b. Goole, e. Bradford, Yorks, 16/188, Pte., k. in a., F. & F., 1/7/16.

Barker, Herbert, b. Bradford, e. Bradford, Yorks, 16/543, Pte., k. in a., F. & F., 1/7/16.

Barstow, Rawden, b. Cleckheaton, Yorks, e. Bradford, Yorks (Cleckheaton), 16/1547, Pte., d., Home, 13/12/16.

Barton, Fred, b. Kippax, Yorks, e. Leeds, 19382, Pte., k. in a., F. & F., 3/5/17.

Bastow, Frank, b. Bradford, e. Bradford, Yorks, 16/1244, Pte., k. in a., F. & F., 1/7/16.

Batchelor, James, b. Croydon, Surrey, e. London, 10612, Cpl., d. of w., F. & F., 28/2/17.

Batley, Bernard Walton, b. Dewsbury, Yorks, e. Bradford, 16/1228, Pte., d. of w., Home, 8/8/16.

Beanland, Joe, b. Bradford, e. Bradford, Yorks, 38323, Pte., d. of w., F. & F., 3/5/17.

Beard, Joseph, b. Bradfield, Sheffield, e. Sheffield, 11981, Pte., d. of w., F. & F., 10/11/16.

Bell, Clifford, b. Calcutta, India, e. York, 38333, Pte., k. in a., F. & F., 27/2/17.

Bell, Edward, b. Bradford, e. Bradford, Yorks, 16/1065, Cpl., k. in a., F. & F., 1/7/16.

Bellamy, Frank, b. Handsworth, Sheffield, e. Sheffield, 41705, L/Cpl., k. in a., F. & F., 3/5/17, formerly 27942, K.O.Y.L.I.

Bentley, Sargent, b. Low Moor, Bradford, e. Bradford, Yorks, 16/312, Pte., d. of w., F. & F., 4/7/16.

Bimrose, Alfred, e. Leeds (Leeds), 300105, Pte., k. in a., F. & F., 3/5/17.

Blackwell, Arthur, b. Bradford, e. Bradford, Yorks, 16/1147, Pte., d. of w., F. & F., 9/8/16.

Blakeborough, William Herbert, b. Bradford, e. Bradford, Yorks, 16/369, Pte., d. Home, 14/5/15.

Blakey, Percy, b. Bradford, e. Bradford, Yorks, 16/820, Pte., d. of w., F. & F., 24/4/16.

Bond, William, b. Bradford, e. Bradford, Yorks, 16/68, Cpl., k. in a., F. & F., 27/2/17.

Booth, William Crane, b. Valetta, Malta, e. Bradford, Yorks (Bradford), 16/1029, Pte., d. of w., F. & F., 6/7/16.

Bottomley, Wilfred Norman, b. Halifax, e. Halifax, Yorks, 38370, Pte., k. in a., F. & F., 3/5/17.

Bowden, Joseph Frederick, b. Bradford, e. Bradford, Yorks, 16/925, Pte., k. in a., F. & F., 3/5/17.

Bower, John Arthur, b. Low Moor, Bradford, e. Bradford, Yorks, 16/263, k. in a., F. & F., 1/7/16.

Brabant, Edwin Walter, b. America, e. Leyton, London (Uxbridge), 52419, Pte., k. in a., F. & F., 12/4/18, formerly M/282462, A.S.C.

Braithwaite, Massee, b. Leeds, e. Leeds, 35628, Pte., k. in a., F. & F., 3/5/17.

Bramley, William, b. Halifax, e. Halifax, Yorks, 29291, Pte., k. in a., F. & F., 3/5/17.

Brayshaw, William Alan, b. Rylstone Skipton, Yorks, e. Bradford, 16/1391, Pte., d., Home, 20/10/15.

Briggs, Albert, b. Clayton, Bradford, e. Bradford, Yorks, 16/1040, Pte., k. in a., F. & F., 1/7/16.

Broady, Michael, b. Staincliffe, Batley, Yorks, e. Bradford, 16/1628, Pte., k. in a., F. & F., 1/7/16.

Brook, James, b. Elland, Yorks, e. Halifax, Yorks, 40194, Pte., k. in a., F. & F., 13/11/16.

Buckborough, James Ernest, b. Bradford, e. Bradford, Yorks, 16/104, Pte., k. in a., F. & F., 1/7/16.

Buckley, Albert, b. Manningham, Bradford, Yorks, e. Bradford, 16/410, Pte., k. in a., F. & F., 1/7/16.

Bunclark, Walter Ernest, b. Torquay, Devon, e. Bradford, Yorks, 16/622, Sgt., k. in a., F. & F., 27/2/17.

Burnley, Arthur, b. Idle, Bradford, e. Bradford, Yorks, 16/1585, Pte., k. in a., F. & F., 1/7/16.

Burrows, John, b. Bradford, e. Bradford, Yorks, 16/920, Sgt., d. of w., F. & F., 7/5/16.

Busfield, Whitehead, e. Pateley Bridge, Yorks, 32002, Pte., k. in a., F. & F., 13/11/16.

Calvert, Albert, b. Bradford, e. Bradford, Yorks, 16/381, Pte., d., F. & F., 28/11/18.

Carter, Jabez, b. Gomersal, Yorks, e. Liversedge, Yorks, 38796, Pte., k. in a., F. & F., 3/5/17.

Cartwright, Ned, b. Heckmondwike, Yorks, e. Bradford, 16/1572, Pte., k. in a., F. & F., 27/2/17.

Catlow, James William, b. Bingley, Yorks, e. Bradford, 16/1627, Pte. k. in a., F. & F., 27/2/17.

Cawthra, Arthur, b. Bradford, e. Bradford, Yorks, 26102, Pte., k. in a., F. & F., 9/11/16.

Chapman, Ernest, b. Bradley, Yorks, e. Huddersfield, 38308, Pte., k. in a., F. & F., 27/2/17.

Chilton, James, b. Kirby Fleetham, Yorks, e. York, 28145, Pte., d. of w., F. & F., 14/6/17.

Clayton, Ernest, b. Featherstone, Yorks, e. Doncaster, 40857, Pte., k. in a., F. & F., 29/7/17.

Clement, John Henry, b. Sheffield, e. Leeds, 24533, Pte., k. in a., F. & F., 13/11/16.

Clough, Squire, b. Bradford, e. Bradford, Yorks, 16/707, Cpl., k. in a., F. & F., 1/7/16.

Cockroft, William, b. Bradford, e. Bradford, Yorks, 16/1170, Pte., k. in a., F & F., 1/7/16.

Coe, Harold Glover, b. Pudsey, Yorks, e. Bradford, 16/130, Pte., k. in a., F. & F., 1/7/16.

Coles, Gerald Irvin, b. York, e. York, 37461, Pte., k. in a., F. & F., 3/5/17.

Constable, Alfred, b. Bradford, e. Bradford, Yorks, 16/514, L/Cpl., d. of w., F. & F., 27/6/16.

Cooper, Ernest, b. Elvington, Yorks, e. York, 32301, Pte., d., F. & F., 17/6/17.

Cooper, George, b. Bradford, e. Bradford, Yorks, 16/1443, Pte., k. in a. F. & F., 1/7/16.

Cope, Edward, b. Queensbury, Bradford, Yorks, e. Bradford, 16/249, Sgt., k. in a., F. & F., 3/5/17.

Core, Arthur, b. Skipton, Yorks, e. Keighley, Yorks, 28746, Pte., k. in a., F. & F., 3/5/17.

Cording, John, b. Featherstone, Yorks, e. Featherstone, 43073, Pte., k. in a., F. & F., 21/7/17.

Cousins, Arthur, b. Sherburn-in-Elmet, Yorks, e. York, 19212, Pte., k. in a., F. & F., 27/7/17.

Crabtree, Leonard, b. Halifax, e. Bradford, Yorks, 16/609, Pte., k. in a., F. & F., 1/7/16.

Craig, Archibald, b. Stornaway, Ross, e. Fort George, Scotland, 16/1734, Pte., k. in a., F. & F., 3/5/17.

Craven, George Willie, b. Saddleworth, Yorks, e. Bradford, 16/806, Pte., k. in a., F. & F., 1/7/16.

Creek, Clifford, b. Leeds, e. Leeds, 38812, Pte., k. in a., F. & F., 5/12/17.

Creek, Luther, b. Keighley, Yorks, e. Bradford, 16/1240, Pte., d. of w., F. & F., 7/7/16.

Cromwell, Garfield, b. Bradford, e. Bradford, Yorks, 16/475, Pte., k. in a., F. & F., 1/7/16.

Crossland, Harry b. Bradford, e. Bradford, Yorks, 16/991, L/Cpl., k. in a., F. & F., 3/5/17.

Cryer, John Henry Ernest, b. Halifax, Yorks, e. Bradford, 16/863, Pte., k. in a., F. & F., 1/7/16.

Culling, William Alfred, b. Bradford, e. Bradford, Yorks, 16/904, Sgt., k. in a., F. & F., 27/7/16.

Cummins, George Henry, b. Whitby, e. Whitby, Yorks, 17168, Pte., k. in a., F. & F., 3/5/17.

Dadswell, Hugh Cecil, b. Wallingford, e. Bradford, Yorks, 16/397, Sgt., k. in a., F. & F., 1/7/16.

Dane, James Arthur, b. Liverpool, e. Bradford, Yorks, 16/821, Sgt., k. in a., F. & F., 3/5/17.

Dargue, Herbert, b. Dewsbury, e. Bradford, Yorks, 16/1043, L/Cpl., d., F. & F., 6/5/17.

Davies, Ernest Jones, b. Pontefract, e. Bradford, Yorks, 16/177, Pte., k. in a., F. & F., 13/8/16.

Davis, Ernest Warr, b. Enfield, Middlesex, e. Pontefract, Yorks, 41667, Pte., d. of w., F. & F., 5/5/17, formerly 39625, K.O.Y.L.I.

Dawson, Thomas, b. Easby, Gt. Ayrton, Yorks, e. York, 38079, Pte., k. in a., F. & F., 3/5/17.

Day, Ernest, b. Leeds, e. Leeds, 37521, Pte., k. in a., F. & F., 21/7/17.

Deakin, Albert John, b. Kempsey, Worcs, e. Bradford, Yorks, 20/96, Cpl., k. in a., F. & F., 27/2/17.

Dearden, Ernest, b. Birdwell, Barnsley, Yorks, e. Bradford (Bradford, Yorks), 16/283, Pte., d. of w., F. & F., 21/8/16.

Dixon, Parrington, b. Dent, Yorks, e. Bradford, Yorks, 16/391, Pte., k. in a., F. & F., 1/7/16.

Douglas, Charles, b. South Shields, e. Piccadilly, London, 38591, Pte., k. in a., F. & F., 27/2/17.

Dowson, John, b. Whitby, Yorks, e. Bradford, Yorks, 16/1198, Pte., k. in a., F. & F., 1/7/16.

Duce, Walter b. Bradford, e. Bradford, Yorks, 16/1084, Pte., k. in a., F. & F., 1/7/16.

Duncan, Thomas Thompson, b. Middlesborough, e. Bradford, Yorks, 16/462, Pte., k. in a., F. & F., 1/7/16.

Durkin, Martin, b. Bradford, e. Bradford, Yorks, 20/219, Pte., d. of w., F. & F. 29/7/16.

Eades, William, b. St. Peters, Birmingham, e. Birmingham, 14344, Pte., k. in a., F. & F., 19/8/17.

Easterby, Albert, b. Bradford, e. Bradford, 16/745, Pte., k. in a., F. & F., 1/7/16.

Edmondson, Willie, b. Bradford, e. Bradford, Yorks (Manningham, Yorks), 16/902, Pte., d. of w., Home, 11/11/16.

Ellis, Francis Wilfred, b. Bradford, e. Bradford, Yorks, 16/1591, Pte., k. in a., F. & F., 27/6/16.

Ellis, John Cyril, b. Bradford, e. Bradford, Yorks (West Bowling, Bradford), 16/954, Pte., d. of w., F. & F., 5/7/16.

Elson, Charles Robert, b. Burton-on-Trent, e. Bradford, Yorks, 16/1484, Pte., d. of w., F. & F., 12/6/16.

Emery, John William, b. Fenton, Staffs, e. Lichfield, 23721, Pte., d. of w., F. & F., 22/7/17.

Endersby, Harold, b. Farsley, Yorks, e. Leeds, 15/1518, Pte., k. in a., F. & F., 3/5/17.

England, William, b. Leeds, e. Leeds, 21435, Pte., k. in a., F. & F., 3/5/17.

Essex, Henry, b. Hull, e. Leeds, 31963, Pte., k. in a., F. & F., 10/11/16.

Fallon, Charles Henry, b. Bradford, e. Bradford, Yorks, 18/554, Pte., k. in a., F. & F., 3/5/17.

Farrar, Charles, b. Bradford, e. Bradford, Yorks, 16/637, Sgt., d, of w., F. & F., 2/3/17, D.C.M.

Fawthorpe, Harold, b. Bradford, e. Bradford, Yorks, 16/642, Pte., k. in a., F. & F., 1/7/16.

Feather, Henry, b. Keighley, e. Bradford, Yorks, 16/387, Cpl., k. in a., F. & F., 27/2/17.

Fenton, Arthur, b. Bradford, e. Bradford, Yorks, 16/239, Pte., k. in a., F. & F., 1/7/16.

Fenwick, Richard, b. Hull, e. York, 6130, Pte., k. in a., F. & F., 3/5/17.

Fethney, Harry, b. Bradford, e. Bradford, Yorks, 18/1420, L/Cpl., k. in a., F. & F., 1/7/16.

Fielden, John, b. Todmorden, Yorks, e. Halifax, 40225, Pte., k. in a., F. & F., 3/5/17.

Flatters, John Crowther, b. Wombwell, Yorks, e. Thorne, Doncaster, Yorks, 28497, Pte., k. in a., F. & F., 3/5/17.

Forder, Alfred, b. King's Lynn, Norfolk, e. Bradford, Yorks (Bradford), 16/921, Pte., k. in a., F. & F., 1/7/16.

Foster, Edwin, b. Halifax, Yorks, e. Bradford (Bradford, Yorks), 16/530, Pte., k. in a., F. & F., 1/7/16.

Foster, William, b. Birstall, Yorks, e. Bradford (Batley, Yorks), 20/93, Cpl., k. in a., F. & F., 5/12/17.

Fowler, George Haughton, b. Bradford, e. Bradford, Yorks, 16/1354, Pte., k. in a., F. & F., 1/7/16.

Fox, John Henry, b. Holbeck, Leeds, e. Huddersfield, Yorks (Leeds), 38362, Pte., k. in a., F. & F., 3/5/17.

Friend, Albert Edward, b. Shorncliffe, Kent, e. York (York), 32815, Pte., k. in a., F. & F., 13/5/17.

Frost, James William, b. Barnsley, Yorks, e. Cleckheaton Yorks, 16/1666, Pte., k. in a., F. & F., 1/7/16.

Fuller, George, b. Bradford, e. Bradford, Yorks, 16/1434, Pte., k. in a., F. & F., 1/7/16.

Galley, Alfred, b. Leeds, e. Leeds, 17124, Pte., k. in a., F. & F., 27/2/17.

Garbutt, Alfred Welburn, b. Leeds, e. York, 38675, Pte., k in a., F. & F., 27/2/17.

Garbutt, William, b. York, e. Bradford, Yorks, 16/1629, Pte., k. in a., F & F., 2/12/16.

Gatehouse, Fred, b. Leeds, e. Huddersfield, Yorks, 16/1577, Pte., d. of w., F. & F., 3/7/16.

Gaunt, Jonas. b. Leeds, e Leeds, 33435, Pte., k. in a., F. & F., 27/2/17.

Gee, Fred, b. Drighlington, Bradford, Yorks, e. Bradford, 16/674, L/Cpl., k. in a., F. & F., 1/7/16.

Gibson, Albert, b. Wakefield, Yorks, e. Leeds, 29529, Pte., k. in a., F. & F., 12/5/17.

Gibson, John Robert, b. Leeds, e. Leeds, 31965, Pte., k. in a., F. & F., 13/11/16.

Gilgan, James, b. Bradford, e. Bradford, Yorks, 16/947, Pte., d. of w., F. & F., 3/11/16.

Gledhill, John Taylor, b. Golcar, Yorks, e. Huddersfield, 40858, Pte., d., F. & F., 24/7/17, formerly, 29/706, Northumberland Fusiliers.

Grainge, Edmund, b. Bradford, e. Bradford, Yorks, 16/834, Pte., d. of w., F. & F., 13/6/16.

Granger, William, b. York, e. York, 36533, Pte., d., F. & F., 15/3/17.

Gratwick, Albert, b. Osbaldwick, Yorks, e. York, 38619, Pte., d. of w., F. & F., 18/8/17.

Graves, Cecil, b. Horsforth, Yorks, e. Bradford, Yorks, 16/424, Cpl., k. in a., F. & F., 27/2/17.

Gray, Gerald, b. Bradford, e. Bradford, Yorks, 16/886, Pte., d., Home, 18/1/15.

Green, Albert Edward, b. Leeds, e. Leeds, 37480, Pte., k. in a., F. & F., 27/2/17.

Green, Thomas, b. Mitcham, Surrey, e. Huddersfield, Yorks, 38307, Pte., k. in a., F. & F., 27/2/17.

Greenhough, Frank, b. Bradford, e. Halifax, Yorks, 40195, Rflmn., d. of w., F. & F., 6/3/17.

Greenwood, Arthur, b. Manningham, Bradford, e. Bradford, Yorks, 16/953, Pte., k. in a., F. & F., 1/7/16.

Greenwood, Bernard, b. Cornholme, Lancs, e. Todmorden, Yorks, 38022, Pte., k. in a., F. & F., 27/2/17.

Gregory, Norman Knight, b. Saltaire, Yorks, e. Bradford, 16/1288, A/Sgt., k. in a., F. & F., 12/5/17.

Grist, Charles, e. Sheffield (Sheffield), 16201, Pte., d., F. & F., 3/5/17, formerly 15190, East Yorks Regt.

Hainsworth, Leonard, b. Farsley, Leeds, e. York, 15481, Pte., k. in a., F. & F., 25/2/17.

Hale, Walter, b. Yeadon, Bradford, e. Bradford, Yorks, 16/828, Pte., k. in a., F. & F., 3/5/17.

Hall, Arthur, b. Leeds, e. Leeds, 37316, Pte., k. in a., F. & F., 27/2/17.

Hall, Joseph, b. Oakworth, Yorks, e. Keighley, Yorks, 16/1684, Pte., k. in a., F. & F., 1/7/16.

Halmshaw, Joseph, b. Cleckheaton, e. Cleckheaton, Yorks, 16/1474, Pte., k. in a., F. & F., 1/7/16.

Hamp, Frederick John, b. East Claydon, Winslow, Bucks, e. Harrogate, 12621, L/Cpl., k. in a., F. & F., 21/7/17.

Hand, Edgar, b. Bradford, e. Bradford, Yorks, 16/868, Pte., k. in a., F. & F., 3/7/16.

Hannan, Arthur, b. Leeds, e. Leeds, 35277, Pte., k. in a., F. & F., 27/2/17.

Hanson, Albert, b. Barnsley, Yorks, e. Bradford, Yorks, 16/1490, Pte., k. in a., F. & F., 1/7/16.

Hanson, Albert, b. Halifax, e. Halifax, Yorks, 32516, Pte., d. of w., F. & F., 12/5/17.

Hanson, Brinton, b. Bradford, e. Bradford, Yorks, 16/824, Sgt., k. in a., F. & F., 9/11/16.

Harbron, Albert, b. Bradford, e. Bradford, Yorks, 16/1145, Pte., k. in a., F. & F., 1/7/16.

Hardwick, Eldred, b. Halton, Leeds, e. Leeds, 14061, Pte., k. in a., F. & F., 3/5/17.

Hardy, Herbert, b. Bradford, e. Bradford, Yorks, 16/1161, Pte., k. in a., F. & F., 27/2/17.

Hargrave, Charles, b. Leeds, e. Leeds, 32840, Pte., d. of w., F. & F., 2/5/17.

Hargreaves, Thomas Edward, b. Bradford, e. Bradford, Yorks, 16/1568, Pte., k. in a., F. & F., 1/7/16.

Harris, Frederick, b. St. Pancras, London, e. London, 35957, Pte., d., Home, 29/12/16.

Harrison, George Tate, b. Bradford, e. Bradford, Yorks, 16/1233, L/Cpl., k. in a., F. & F., 13/11/16.

Harrison, Philip James, b. Tealby, Lincs, e. Bradford, Yorks, 16/1001, Pte., k. in a., F. & F., 1/7/16.

Harrison, Willie, b. Bradford, e. Bradford, Yorks, 16/804, Sgt., k. in a., 27/2/17.

Hart, Ted Edward, b. Hackney, London, e. Finsbury Park, London, 20/302, Pte., k. in a., F. & F., 3/5/17, formerly 22180, Suffolk Regt.

Hartley, George Thomas, b. Hebden Bridge, Yorks, e. Halifax, Yorks, 38102, Pte., k. in a., F. & F., 27/2/17.

Hartley, James, b. Oswaldtwistle, Lancs, e. Halifax, Yorks (Barnoldswick), 38110, Pte., k. in a., F. & F., 27/2/17.

Hartley, Walter, b. Bradford, e. Bradford, Yorks (Clayton-le-Moors, Accrington), 16/232, Pte., k. in a., F. & F., 1/7/16.

Hatfield, Herbert, b. York, e. York, 37533, Pte., k. in a., F. & F., 3/5/17.

Hawkesworth, Richard, b. Hunslet, Leeds, e. Bradford, Yorks (Bradford), 16/167, Sgt., k. in a., F. & F., 1/7/16.

Haxby, Lofthouse, b. Armley, Leeds, e. Leeds, 12722, Pte., k. in a., F. & F., 3/5/17.

Heyes, Nathan, b. Leeds, e. Leeds, 3/9260, Pte., k. in a., F. & F., 3/5/17.

Hirst, John Wade, b. Leeds, e. Bradford, Yorks (Bradford), 16/1452, Pte., d. of w., F. & F., 5/7/16.

Hodgson, Alfred, b. Clayton, Bradford, e. Bradford, Yorks, 16/926, Pte., k. in a., F. & F., 1/7/16.

Hodgson, James Frederick, b. Bradford, e. Bradford Yorks, 16/733, Pte., k. in a., F. & F., 11/8/16.

Holdsworth, Arthur, b. Lincoln, e. Lincoln, 40423, Pte., k. in a., F. & F., 3/5/17, formerly 3228, 4th Lincolnshire Regt.

Holdsworth, Harry, b. Bradford, e. Halifax, Yorks, 32158, Pte., k. in a., F. & F., 27/2/17.

Holgate, William Arthur, b. Sawley, Clitheroe, Yorks, e. Keighley. Yorks, 28522, Pte., d., F. & F., 29/12/18.

Holmes, Clough, b. Bradford, e. Bradford, Yorks, 16/1121, Pte., k. in a., F. & F., 1/7/16.

Holmes, Wilfred, b. Addingham, Yorks, e. Bradford, Yorks (Bradford), 16/713, Pte., k. in a., F. & F., 1/7/16.

Horn, Dawson, b. Leyburn, Northallerton, Yorks, e. Bradford, Yorks (Bradford), 16/865, Pte., k. in a., F. & F., 1/7/16.

Horsfall, Fred, b. Saltaire, Yorks, e. Bradford, Yorks, 16/1442, Pte., k. in a., F. & F., 27/2/17.

Horsfall, Tom, b. Shipley, Yorks, e. Bradford, Yorks, 16/535, Pte., k. in a., F. & F., 1/7/16.

Howard, Ernest, b. Bowling, Bradford, Yorks, e. Bradford, 16/998, L/Cpl., k. in a., F. & F., 1/7/16.

Howarth, George, b. Bradford, e. Bradford, Yorks, 16/1016, Pte., k. in a., F. & F., 1/7/16.

Howden, Sidney, b. Liverton, Lincs, e. Holbeach (Holbeach), 40426, Pte., k. in a., F. & F., 27/2/17, formerly 4682, Lincs Regt.

Hunt, William Denis, b. Garforth, Leeds, e. Bradford, Yorks, 16/420, Pte., d. of w., F. & F., 13/11/16.

Hurp, Edward, b. Bradford, e. Bradford, Yorks, 16/47, Sgt., k. in a., F. & F., 27/2/17.

Hutchison, Louis, b. Leeds, e. Leeds, 24815, Pte., d. of w., F. & F., 16/11/16.

Illingworth, Henry, b. Bradford, e. Bradford, Yorks, 16/95, Pte., d., Home, 30/12/14.

Irving, Frank, b. Bradford, e. Bradford, Yorks, 16/152, Pte., d. of w., F. & F., 10/11/16.

Irving, Wilfred, b. Little Woodhouse, Yorks, e. Halifax, Yorks, 40215, Pte., k. in a., F. & F., 9/11/16.

Ives, Mark Mountain, e. Leeds (Bramley, Yorks), 40203, Pte., k. in a., F. & F., 27/2/17.

Jackson, Horace, b. St. Mary's, Lincoln, e. Birmingham, 15515, Pte., k. in a., F. & F., 27/2/17.

Jackson, Wilfred, b. Bradford, e. Bradford, Yorks, 16/195, Pte., d. of w., F. & F., 12/7/16.

Jagger, Wilfred, b. Leeds, e. Leeds, 28892, Pte., k. in a., F. & F., 27/2/17.

James, John, b. Cheadle, Staffs, e. Pontefract, Yorks, 14796, L/Cpl., d. of w., F. & F., 6/6/17.

Jarvis, Arthur William, e. Spalding, Lincs (Spalding, Lincs), 40427, Pte., k. in a., F. & F., 3/5/17, formerly 4303, 4th Lincs Regt.

Jarvis, Charles, b. Rotherham, Yorks, e. Chapeltown (Ecclesfield, Sheffield), 18477, Pte., d. of w., F. & F., 30/7/17.

Jeffery, Thomas Frederick, b. Plymouth, Devon, e. Bradford, Yorks (Bradford), 40824, Pte., k. in a., F. & F., 3/5/17.

Johns, Samuel, b. Leeds, e. Leeds, 23798, Pte., k. in a., F. & F., 27/2/17.

Johnson, Alfred, b. Barrow-on-Humber, e. Bradford, Yorks, 16/217, Pte., k. in a., F. & F., 1/7/16.

Johnson, Henry Martin Finch, b. Highbury, London, e. Bradford, Yorks (Eccleshill, Bradford), 16/362, Cpl., k. in a., F. & F., 1/7/16.

Jones, George, b. Salford, Lancs, e. Manchester, 10193, L/Cpl., k. in a., F. & F., 27/10/16.

Jones, Tom Lancelot, b. Liverpool, e. Liverpool, 37651, Pte., k. in a., F. & F., 3/5/17, formerly 117979, R.F.A.

Jordan, Walter, b. Leeds, e. Bradford, Yorks, 16/1186, Pte., k. in a., F. & F., 1/7/16.

Jowett, Charles, b. Leeds, e. Leeds, 38783, Pte., k. in a., F. & F., 3/5/17.

Jowett, Harry, b. Howarth, Yorks, e. Bradford, 16/1368, Pte., k. in a., F. & F., 1/7/16.

Keighley, Clifford, b. Leeds, e. Leeds, 24199, Cpl., k. in a., F. & F., 27/2/17.

Kelsey, Percy, b. Peak Forest, Derbyshire, e. Chapel-en-le-Frith (Dove Holes), 40400, L/Cpl., k. in a., F. & F., 25/2/17, formerly 53475, Lincs Regt.

Kellett, James, b. Gildersome, Yorks, e. Leeds, 300077, Pte., d. of w., F. & F., 6/5/17.

Kendrick, Fred., b. Dewsbury, Yorks, e. Bradford (Shipley, Yorks), 16/1262, Pte., k. in a., F. & F., 1/7/16.

Kenningham, Edgar, b. Bradford, e. Bradford, Yorks, 18/771, L/Cpl., k. in a., F. & F., 1/7/16.

Kenny, William, b. Bradford, e. Bradford, Yorks, 16/336, Pte., d. of w., F. & F., 7/7/16.

Kershaw Frederick Percy, b. Bradford, e. Bradford, Yorks, 16/415, Pte., k. in a., F. & F., 1/7/16.

Kilvington, Charles, b. York, e. Leeds (Leeds), 32298, Pte., k. in a., F. & F., 27/2/17.

King, Herbert, b. Wakefield, Yorks, e. Leeds, 32307, Pte., k. in a., F. & F., 9/11/16.

Kirkman, Harry, b. Bradford, e. Bradford, Yorks, 16/1189, Pte., d., F. & F., 20/11/16.

Kitchingman, Norris, b. Ripon, Yorks, e. Bradford, 16/248, Pte., k. in a., F. & F., 19/5/16.

Knight, Rowland Hebden, b. Allerton, Bradford, Yorks, e. Bradford, 16/737, Pte., k. in a., F. & F., 1/7/16.

Ladley, Charles William, b. Sowerby Bridge, Yorks, e. Leeds, 38678, Pte., k. in a., F. & F., 27/2/17.

Lamberton, John Thomas, b. Felling, Gateshead, e. Newcastle-on-Tyne (Windy Nook, Durham), 16007, Pte., k. in a., F. & F., 3/5/17.

Lassey, Willie, b. Bradford, e. Bradford, Yorks, 16/29, Pte., d. of w., F. & F., 16/5/16.

Latham, Percy George, b. Bradford, e. Bradford, Yorks, 16/156, C.S.M., k. in a., F. & F., 1/7/16.

Laycock, Harry, b. Manningham, Bradford, e. Bradford, Yorks, 16/550, Pte., k. in a., F. & F., 3/5/17.

Leach, Ernest, b. Bradford, e. Bradford, Yorks, 16/198, Pte., k. in a., F. & F., 1/7/16.

Leach, Eddy, b. Bradford, e. Bradford, Yorks, 16/531, Pte., k in a., F. & F., 1/7/16.

Ledger, Joseph Henry, b. Carbrook, Sheffield, e. Attercliffe, Sheffield, 22587, Pte., k. in a., F. & F., 1/7/16, formerly 24906 K.O.Y.L.I.

Leech, George Edward, b. Bradford, e. Bradford, Yorks, 16/749, Pte., k. in a., F. & F., 1/7/16.

Leeming, Henry Richard, b. Giggleswick, Yorks, e. Keighley, 20/146, Pte., k. in a., F. & F., 29/7/16.

Leeming, Jonas Manasseh, b. Eccleshill, Bradford, e. Bradford, Yorks, 16/1511, Pte., k. in a., F. & F., 1/7/16.

Leigh, Ernest Kirkham, b. Darwin, Lancs, e. Barnoldswick, Yorks (Barnoldswick), 20/188, Pte., k. in a., F. & F., 29/7/16.

Leonard, Harry, b. Huddersfield, e. Huddersfield, 38358, Pte., k. in a., F. & F., 3/5/17.

Lightowler, Willie, b. Bradford, e. Bradford, Yorks, 20/24, Pte., k. in a., F. & F., 1/7/16.

Lingard, Thomas, b. Bradford, e. Bradford, Yorks, 16/175, Pte., k. in a., F. & F., 1/7/16.

Linley, Abraham, b. Leeds, e. Bradford, Yorks, 16/1677, Pte., k. in a., F. & F., 1/7/16.

Little, Henry Arnold, b. Bradford, e. Bradford, Yorks, 16/413, L/Sgt., k. in a., F. & F., 27/2/17.

Lockett, John, b. Bradford, e. Bradford, Yorks, 16/199, Pte., k. in a., F. & F., 1/7/16.

Longster, Thomas George, e. Leeds (Leeds), 300118, Rfln., d. of w., F. & F., 14/5/17.

Lowe, Bertie, b. Workington, Cumberland, e. Bradford, Yorks, 16/1673, Pte., k. in a., F. & F., 1/7/16.

Lumb, Mark, b. Batley, Yorks, e. Batley, 43764, Pte., k. in a., F. & F., 3/5/17, formerly 28326, K.O.Y.L.I.

Lumb, Matthew, b. Halifax, e. Halifax, 41309, Pte., k. in a., F. & F., 3/5/17.

Lynch, Joseph, b. Leeds, e. Leeds, 34004, Pte., d., F. & F., 7/10/17.

McConnell, William, b. Kirkinner, Wigtownshire, e. Bradford, Yorks, 16357, L/Cpl., k. in a., F. & F., 27/7/16.

McCormack, George Alexander, b. Bradford, e. Bradford, Yorks, 16/318, Cpl., k. in a., F. & F., 3/5/17.

McDermott, Frederick, b. Wooburn, Bucks, e. Bradford (Bradford), 16/560, Pte., k. in a., F. & F., 1/7/16.

McGuire, Thomas Osbourne, b. Boston, e. Boston, Lincs, 40414, L/Cpl., k. in a., F. & F., 27/2/17, formerly 4586, Lincolnshire Regt.

McIntyre, Arthur, b. Filey, Yorks, e. Bradford (Long Preston), 16/229, Cpl., k. in a., F. & F., 27/2/17.

McMahon, John Thomas, b. Batley, Yorks, e. Bradford, 16/1509, Pte., k. in a., F. & F., 1/7/16.

McMurrough, Robert, b. Sunderland, e. Sunderland, 4/8176, Pte., d. of w., F. & F., 28/2/17.

Mackay, Edford, b. Wibsey, Bradford, e. Bradford, Yorks, 16/908, Pte., d. of w., F. & F., 10/5/16.

Mair, Fred Sutherland, b. Leeds, e. Leeds, 32407, L/Cpl., k. in a., F. & F., 27/2/17.

Mallinson, Albert, b. Bradford, e. Bradford, Yorks, 16/704, Pte., k. in a., F. & F., 1/7/16.

Manley, John, b. Bradford Moor, Bradford, e. Bradford, Yorks, 16/913, Sgt., k. in a., F. & F., 3/5/17.

Mann, Albert James, b. Spa, Norfolk, e. York, 36570, Pte., d., F. & F., 28/5/17.

Marsden, Ben, b. Bradford, e. Bradford, Yorks, 16/1241, Pte., k. in a., F. & F., 1/7/16.

Marston, James, b. Bradford, e. Bradford, Yorks, 16/1277, L/Cpl., k. in a., F. & F., 1/7/16.

Martin, Albert, b. Wickham Skeith, Eye, Suffolk, e. York, 4/8150, Pte., k. in a., F. & F., 29/7/17.

Martin, John, b. Richmond, Yorks, e. Richmond, 22010, Pte., k. in a., F. & F., 27/2/17.

Martindale, Irvin, b. Bradford, e. Bradford, Yorks, 16/1297, Pte., k. in a., F. & F., 1/7/16.

Martindale, Maurice, b. Manningham, Yorks, e. Bradford, Yorks (Heaton, Bradford), 16/319, Pte., k. in a., F. & F., 1/7/16.

Mason, Riley, e. Pontefract, Yorks (Morley, Yorks), 41708, Pte., d. of w., F. & F., 13/5/17.

May, Clement, b. Keighley, Yorks, e. Leeds, 32857, Pte., d. of w., F. & F., 13/11/16.

May, William, b. Bradford, e. Bradford, Yorks, 16/1437, Pte., d. of w., Home, 9/7/16.

Metcalfe, Thomas William, b. Shipton, Yorks, e. York (York), 38332, Pte., k. in a., F. & F., 27/2/17.

Midgley, Verity, b. Bradford, e. Bradford, Yorks, 16/518, L/Cpl., k. in a., F. & F., 1/7/16.

Midgley, Walter, b. Keighley, e. Keighley, Yorks, 32633, Pte., k. in a., F. & F., 3/5/17.

Miller, Frederick Harold, b. Markington, Yorks, e. Ripon, Yorks, 40827, Pte., k. in a., F. & F., 3/5/17.

Mills, John William, b. Bradford, e. Bradford, Yorks, 16/399, Pte., k. in a., F. & F., 1/7/16.

Moffatt, Seth Shaw, b. Newcastle, e. Newcastle (Benwell, Newcastle), 41707, Pte., k. in a., F. & F., 27/2/17, formerly 40960, 3rd K.O.Y.L.I.

Mooney, Joseph, b. Bradford, e. Bradford, Yorks, 16/735, Sgt., k. in a., F. & F., 13/11/16.

Moore, Ernest, b. Derby, e. Doncaster, Yorks, 41670, Pte., d. of w., Home, 5/5/17, formerly 34262, K.O.Y.L.I.

Moore, John, b. Bradford, e. Bradford, Yorks, 16/1423, Pte., k. in a., F. & F., 1/7/16.

Moore, Joe, b. Bradford, e. Bradford, Yorks, 16/892, Pte., k. in a., F. & F., 27/7/16.

Morgan, William, b. Bradford, e. Bradford, Yorks, 16/8, Sgt., k. in a., F. & F., 1/7/16.

Morritt, Walter, b. Leeds, e. Leeds, 32852, Pte., k. in a., F. & F., 3/5/17.

Morton, James, b. Heckmondwike, Yorks, e. Bradford, 16/1488, Pte., k. in a., F. & F., 27/2/17.

Mosley, William Arthur, b. Bradford, e. Bradford, Yorks, 16/133, Cpl., k. in a., F. & F., 1/7/16.

Mountain, John Edwin, b. York, e. Acomb, Yorks, 35063, Pte., k. in a., F. & F., 27/2/17.

Mountain, John William, b. Leeds, e. Leeds, 24708, L./Sgt., d. of w., F. & F., 28/2/17.

Murgatroyd, William, b. Baildon, Yorks, e. Baildon, 38351, Pte., k. in a., F. & F., 3/5/17.

Myers, Thomas Henry, b. Leeds, e. Leeds, 35187, Pte., k. in a., F. & F., 27/2/17.

Muff, Herbert, b. Bradford, e. Bradford, Yorks, 16/1291, Pte., k. in a., F. & F., 28/8/16.

Musgrave, Frank, b. Bradford, e. Bradford, Yorks, 16/762, Pte., k. in a., F. & F., 1/7/16.

Naughton, Francis William, b. York, e. York, Pte., 32947, k. in a., F. & F., 27/2/17.

Naylor, Arthur, b. Leeds, e. Leeds, 40206, Pte., k. in a., F. & F., 27/2/17.

Naylor, Herbert, b. Leeds, e. Leeds, 36807, Pte., k. in a., F. & F., 3/5/17.

Naylor, Reginald Bolton, b. Leeds, e. Leeds, 36772, Pte., d. of w., Home, 8/6/17.

Needham, William Henry, b. Sheffield, e. Sheffield, 36347, Pte., k. in a., F. & F., 27/2/17.

Nelson, Fred, b. Bradford, e. Bradford, Yorks, 16/180, Sgt., k. in a., F. & F., 29/7/17.

Nettleton, Ernest, b. Idle, Bradford, Yorks, e. Bradford, 16/1172, L/Cpl., k. in a., F. & F., 27/2/17.

Newman, Herbert Beaumont, b. Bradford, e. Bradford, Yorks, 16/1100, Pte., k. in a., F. & F., 1/7/16.

Newsholme, Arthur William, b. Bradford, e. Bradford, Yorks, 16/781, L/Cpl., k. in a., F. & F., 27/2/17.

Newton, Alfred Ernest, b. Bingley, Yorks, e. Bradford, Yorks (Bradford), 16/524, Cpl., k. in a., F. & F., 1/7/16.

Newton, James, e. Leeds, 36849, Pte., d., Home, 8/5/17.

Nurse, Herbert Edward, b. Chorlton-on-Medlock, Manchester, e. Bradford, Yorks, 16/967, Pte., d. of w., F. & F., 31/7/17.

Packett, Donald, b. Cullingworth, Bradford, Yorks, e. Bradford, 16/659, Cpl., k. in a., F. & F., 1/7/16.

Palmer, John William, b. Leeds, e. Leeds, 17/1584, Pte., k. in a., F. & F., 27/2/17.

Parker, Tom, b. Bradford, e. Bradford, Yorks, 16/1258, Pte., k. in a., F. & F., 1/7/16.

Parker, Willie, b. Clayton, Bradford, e. Bradford, Yorks, 16/725, Pte., k. in a., F. & F., 1/7/16.

Parkinson, Walter, b. Bradford, Yorks, e. Matlock, Yorks, 19249, Pte., k. in a., F. & F., 2/12/16.

Paterson, Malcolm Bruce, b. Shipley, Yorks, e. Bradford, Yorks, 16/687, Pte., k. in a., F. & F., 1/7/16.

Pearson, Alexander Frederick, b. London, e. Leeds, 40834, Pte., k. in a., F. & F., 27/2/17.

Pearson, James Arthur, b. Bradford, e. Bradford, Yorks, 20/131, Pte., k. in a., F. & F., 29/7/16.

Pearson, Maurice, b. Bradford, e. Bradford, Yorks, 16/1433, Pte., k. in a., F. & F., 1/7/16.

Pearson, Stephen, b. Bradford, e. Bradford, Yorks, 16/1420, Pte., k. in a., F. & F., 1/7/16.

Peck, John William Rowley, b. Bradford, e. Bradford, Yorks, 28690, Pte., k. in a., F. & F., 27/2/17.

Peel, Joseph Edward, b. Heckmondwike, Yorks, e. Liversedge, Yorks, 28679, Pte., k. in a., F. & F., 12/5/17.

Perray, Percy, b. Leeds, e. Leeds, 27850, Pte., k. in a., F. & F., 2/12/16.

Pickup, James Edwin, b. Horton, Bradford, e. Bradford, Yorks, 16/521, L/Cpl., k. in a., F. & F., 1/7/16.

Poole, Samuel, b. Bradford, e. Bradford, Yorks, 16/1037, L/Cpl., k. in a., F. & F., 1/7/16.

Porter, Fred, b. Dudley Hill, Bradford, e. Bradford, Yorks, 16/632, Pte., k. in a., F. & F., 1/7/16.

Potts, Joseph, b. Bradford, e. Bradford, Yorks, 16/1336, Pte., k. in a., F. & F., 1/7/16.

Powell, Ernest, b. Darfield, Barnsley, Yorks, e. Bradford (Bradford, Yorks), 16/509, Pte., k. in a., F. & F., 27/2/17.

Pratt, Ernest, b. Leeds, e. York, 32843, L/Cpl., k. in a., F. & F., 27/2/17.

Prentice, Arthur, b. Tockwith, Yorks, e. Pudsey, 40835, Pte., d., Home, 21/2/18.

Quirk, Thomas, b. Bradford, e. Bradford, 20/114, Pte., d. of w., F. & F., 1/8/16.

Raine, George, b. Shipley, Yorks, e. Bradford, Yorks, 16/691, Pte.,
k. in a., F. & F., 1/7/16.
Ramsden, Herbert, b. Pudsey, Yorks, e. Bradford, Yorks (Bradford),
16/731, Pte., k. in a., F. & F., 1/7/16.
Ratcliffe, Sid, b. Halifax, e. Halifax, Yorks, 40196, Pte., d. of w., F. & F.,
8/5/17.
Rawnsley, Herbert Vincent, b. Clayton, Bradford, e. Bradford, Yorks,
16/1133, Pte., k. in a., F. & F., 1/7/16.
Renshaw, Ernest, b. Shipley, Yorks, e. Bradford, Yorks, 16/513, Pte.,
k. in a., F. & F., 1/7/16.
Reveley, Gordon Reginald, b. St. Stephens, Bradford, e. Bradford,
Yorks, 16/837, Pte., k. in a., F. & F., 18/5/16.
Rhodes, Albert, b. Leeds, e. Leeds, 38782, Pte., d., F. & F., 9/5/17.
Rhodes, Charles, b. Frizinghall, Bradford, e. Bradford, Yorks, 16/964,
Pte., k. in a., F. & F., 1/7/16.
Rhodes, Thomas, b. Thackley, Bradford, e. Bradford, Yorks, 16/1247,
Pte., k. in a., F. & F., 1/7/16.
Rice, Lawrence, b. Bradford, e. Bradford, Yorks, 16/1344, Pte., k. in a.,
F. & F., 1/7/16.
Ridley, Fred, b. York, e. Bradford, Yorks (Bradford), 16/1428, Pte.,
k. in a., F. & F., 1/7/16.
Ridley, Frederick Birkett, b. Aspatria, Cumberland, e. Leeds (Armley,
Leeds), 35294, Pte., k. in a., F. & F., 27/2/17.
Roach, Thomas, e. Leeds (Leeds), 300076, L/Cpl., k. in a., F. & F.,
3/5/17.
Roberts, John, b. Leeds, e. Yorks, 38643, Pte., k. in a., F. & F., 30/4/17.
Robertson, John Bright, b. Stirling, Scotland, e. Bradford, Yorks, 16/123,
Pte., d. of w., F. & F., 3/7/16.
Robinson, Ernest, b. Bradford, e. Bradford, Yorks, 16/874, Pte., d. of w.,
F. & F., 12/5/17.
Robinson, Frederick William, b. Burley-in-Wharfedale, Yorks, e. Brad-
ford (Manningham, Bradford, Yorks), 16/1326, Pte., d. of w.,
F. & F., 10/7/16.
Robinson, Horace, b. Wakefield, Yorks, e. Bradford (Bradford, Yorks),
16/1242, Pte., k. in a., F. & F., 3/5/17.
Robinson, James William, e. Shipley, Yorks, 38293, Pte., d. of w.,
Home, 3/4/17.

Robinson, Sam, b. Leeds, e. Leeds, 40836, Pte., k. in a., F. & F., 30/4/17.
Robshaw, Charles, b. Barwick-in-Elmet, Yorks, e. Garforth, Leeds,
33220, Pte., k. in a., F. & F., 27/2/17,.
Rogers, Henry Lawrence, b. Bradford, e. Bradford, Yorks, 16/340,
Pte., k. in a., F & F., 1/7/16.
Rogers, Joseph, b. Skipton, Yorks, e. Skipton, 28740, Pte., d. of w.,
F. & F., 2/5/17.
Rowland, Robert, b. Bradford, e. Bradford, Yorks, 16/1398, Pte.,
k. in a., F. & F. 1/7/16.
Rudd, Joseph, b. Bradford, e. Bradford, Yorks, 16/663, Pte., k. in a.,
F. & F. 2/12/16.
Rudd, Percy, b. West Bowling, Bradford, e. Bradford, Yorks, 16/307,
Pte., d., F. & F. 22/10/18.
Rushworth, William, b. Bradford, e. Bradford, Yorks, 16/246, Pte.,
k. in a., F. & F., 15/8/16.
Rust, Walter, b. Bradford, e. Bradford, Yorks, 19/130, Pte., d., F. & F.,
9/11/16.
Ryan, Bernard, b. Leeds, e. Leeds, 14980, Pte., k. in a., F. & F., 3/9/16.
Saunders, James Henry, b. Bradford, Yorks, e. Bradford, 16/701, Pte.,
d. of w., F. & F., 7/8/16.
Sayers, John James, b. Bradford, Yorks, e. Bradford, Yorks, 16/1293,
Pte., k. in a., F. & F., 1/7/16.
Scarth, George, b. Leeds, e. Leeds, 37014, Pte., F. & F., 12/2/17.
Schofield, Fred, b. Brighouse, Yorks, e. Halifax, Yorks (Bradford),
40218, Pte., k. in a., F. & F., 3/5/17.
Scott, George, b. York, e. York, 11662, Pte., d. of w., F. & F., 12/5/17.
Scott, Harry, b. Shipley, Yorks, e. Bradford, Yorks, 16/1289, Pte.,
k. in a., F. & F., 1/7/16.
Selby, Christopher, b. Bradford, e. Bradford, Yorks, 16/1399, Pte.,
d. of w., F. & F., 5/7/16.
Senior, Charles, b. Leeds, e. Leeds, 37716, Pte., k. in a., F. & F., 3/5/17.
Senior, Thomas Edward, b. Leeds, e. Leeds, 32405, Pte., k. in a., F. & F.,
27/2/17.
Setterington, Thomas, b. Leeds, e. Tadcaster, Yorks, 33040, Pte.,
d. of w., F. & F., 7/3/17.
Shackleton, Ernest, b. Bradford, e. Bradford, Yorks, 16/825, Pte.,
k. in a., F. & F., 1/7/16.
Sharman, Charles Victor, b. Bradford, e. Bradford, Yorks, 16/370, Pte.,
d. of w., F. & F., 1/8/16.
Sharp, Harold, b. Leeds, e. Leeds, 27214, Pte., k. in a., F. & F., 27/6/17.
Sharpe, Fred, b. Thornton, Yorks, e. Bradford, Yorks, 38291, Pte.,
d. of w., F. & F., 2/3/17.
Shaw, Albert, b. Horton, Bradford, Yorks, e. Bradford, 16/879, Pte.,
d. of w., F. & F., 4/9/16.
Sheldon, Tom, b. Ripon, e. Ripon, Yorks, 23363, L/Cpl., k. in a., F. & F.,
3/5/17.
Shooter, James Robert, b. Low Moor, Yorks, e. Bradford, Yorks,
16/1048, Pte., k. in a., F. & F., 1/7/16.
Shouksmith, Harold Wilson, b. York, e. Leeds, 40845, Pte., k. in a.,
F. & F., 3/5/17.
Sircom, Harry Innerdale, b. Bradford, Yorks, e. Bradford, 16/732, Pte.,
d. of w.. F. & F., 19/6/16.

Skirrow, Harry Edmundson, b. Bradford, Yorks, e. Bradford, 16/914, Pte., d. of w., F. & F., 13/12/16.

Slingsby, Fred, b. Windhill, Bradford, Yorks, e. Bradford, 16/350, Pte., k. in a., F. & F., 23/4/16.

Smales, Joe, b. Rothwell, Leeds, e. Wakefield, Yorks, 28511, Pte., d., F. & F., 3/8/18.

Smith, Arthur, b. Leeds, e. Leeds, 40853, Pte., k. in a., F. & F., 27/2/17.

Smith, Charles, b. Leeds, e. Leeds, 25323, Pte., k. in a., F. & F., 27/2/17.

Smith, Ernest Marsden Conrad, b. Leeds, e. Leeds, 37233, Pte., k. in a., F. & F., 27/2/17.

Smith, Frederick Arthur, b. Shipley, Yorks, e. Bradford, 16/1416, Pte., k. in a., F &. F., 1/7/16.

Smith, John William, b. Nottingham, e. Nottingham, 43844, Pte., k. in a, F. & F., 3/5/17, formerly 30560, Sherwood Foresters.

Smith, Raymond, b. Bradford, Yorks, e. Bradford, 16/21, Pte., k. in a., F. & F, 1/7/16

Smith, Tom, b. Keighley, e. Keighley, Yorks, 16/1674, Pte, k. in a., F. & F, 3/5/17.

Smith, Victor, b. Denholme, Yorks, e. Bradford, 16/269, Pte., k. in a., F. & F., 23/4/16.

Smith, Walter, b. Cleckheaton, Yorks, e. Bradford, 16/451, Pte., d. of w., F. & F., 9/7/16.

Smith, Willie, b. Leeds, e. Leeds, 24153, Pte., k. in a., F. & F., 28/10/16.

Speight, Albert, b. Dewsbury, Yorks, e. Bradford, 16/1430, Pte., k. in a., F. & F., 1/7/16.

Spence, Alfred Brightrick, b. Heaton, Bradford, Yorks, e. Bradford, 16/823, Sgt., k. in a., F. & F., 1/7/16.

Spence, Eric, b. Bradford, Yorks, e. Bradford, 16/466, L/Cpl., k. in a., F. & F., 1/7/16.

Spencer, Francis William, b. Bradford e. Bradford, Yorks, 16/165, Sgt., k. in a., F. & F., 3/5/17.

Spire, Henry Osbourne, b. Bradford, e. Bradford, Yorks, 16/726, L/Cpl., k. in a., F. & F., 1/7/16.

Stables, Walter, b. Horsforth, Yorks, e. Leeds, 24248, Pte., k. in a., F. & F., 3/5/17.

Stakersmith, Wilfred Raymond, e. Selby (Micklefield, Yorks), 38680, Pte., k. in a., F. & F., 27/2/17.

Stamp, Edward John, b. Leeds, e. Leeds, 17198, A/Cpl. k in a., F. & F., 1/7/16.

Stancomb, Bryan Mortimer, b. Bradford, e. Bradford, Yorks, 41317, Pte., d., F. & F., 22/2/17.

Stanney, Thomas Richard, b. Brentford, e. Brentford, Middlesex, 20/323, Pte., d., Home, 25/4/17, formerly 22870, Suffolk Regt.

Stead, John William, b. Goole, Yorks, e. Wakefield, Yorks, 41711, Pte., k. in a., F. & F., 27/2/17, formerly 33952, K.O.Y.L.I.

Stell, Joseph, b. Keighley, e, Keighley, Yorks, 18/1046, L/Cpl., k. in a., F. & F., 1/7/16.

Stephenson, Charles William, b. Leeds, e. Leeds, 37458, Pte., k. in a., F. & F., 3/5/17.

Stephenson, William David, b. Hunslet, Leeds, e. Harrogate (Bradford, Yorks), 4/8430, L/Cpl., k. in a., F. & F., 9/11/16.

Stobart, Fred, b. Lemington, Northumberland, e. Whitley Bay, 59695, Pte. (Accident), F. & F., 6/2/18.

Stockton, Charles, b. Hull, e. Hull, 13944, Pte., k. in a,. F. & F., 3/5/17.

Strawson, Harold, e. Horncastle, 40441, Sgt., k. in a., F. & F., 3/5/17, formerly 3805, Lincoln Regt.

Sugden, Arnold, b. Halifax e. Halifax, Yorks, 28324, Pte., d. of w., F. & F., 22/11/16.

Sutcliffe, Herbert, b. Pudsey, e. Pudsey, Yorks, 32422, Pte., k. in a., F. & F., 9/11/16.

Swinbank, James Allan, b. Bradford, e. Bradford, Yorks, 16/314, Pte., k. in a., F. & F., 9/11/16.

Sykes, Arthur, b. Bradford, e. Bradford, Yorks, 16/1706, Pte., d. of w., F. & F., 1/8/16.

Sykes, Arthur Edward, b. Halifax, Yorks, e., Bradford, Yorks, 16/1448, L/Cpl., k. in a., F. & F., 1/7/16.

Tankard, Herbert, b. Listerhills, Bradford, e. Bradford, Yorks, 16/96, Pte., k. in a., F. & F., 3/5/17.

Tarrant, George, b. Portsmouth, e. Bradford, Yorks, 16/455, L/Cpl., d. of w., F. & F., 12/6/1.

Tasker, Douglas, b. Bradford, e. Bradford, Yorks, 16/1274, Pte., k. in a., F. & F., 1/7/16.

Taylor, Allan, b. Leeds, e. Leeds, 35568, Pte., k. in a., F. & F., 3/5/17.

Taylor, George Stead, b. Bradford, e. Bradford, Yorks, 16/505, Pte., k. in a., F. & F., 1/7/16.

Taylor, Pearson, b. North Rigton, Pannel, Harrogate, Yorks, e. Knaresborough, 33030, Pte., d. of w., F. & F., 5/5/17.

Thackray, Thomas, b. Bradford, e. Bradford, Yorks, 26127, Pte., k. in a., F. & F., 29/7/16.

Thrippleton, Austin, b. Stanningley, Leeds, e. Bradford, Yorks, 16/1266, Pte., k. in a., F. & F., 1/7/16.

Tillett, Henry, b. Tadcaster, e. Tadcaster, Yorks, 32356, Pte., d., F. & F., 3/5/17.

Todd, Walter, b. York, e. York, 28171, Pte., k. in a., F. & F., 3/5/17.

Tolson, Percy, b. Birkenshaw, Bradford, Yorks, e. Bradford, 16/1024, Pte., d. of w., F. & F., 29/9/16.

Tomlinson, Denis, b. Halifax, e. Bradford, Yorks (Bradford), 16/734, Pte., k. in a., F. & F., 1/7/16.

141

Townend, James Arthur, b. Bradford, e. Bradford, Yorks, 16/120, L/Cpl., k. in a., F. & F., 1/7/16.
Towse, Albert, b. Pannel, Yorks, e. Harrogate, 23837, Pte., d., F. & F., 12/3/17.
Underwood, Harry, b. Girlington, Bradford, e. Bradford, Yorks, 16/31, Cpl., k. in a., F. & F., 1/7/16.
Valentine, George Henry, b. Northampton, e. Leeds, 37459, L./Cpl., k. in a., F. & F., 3/5/17.
Waddilove, Norman, b. Bradford, e. Bradford, Yorks, 16/313, Pte., k. in a., F. & F., 1/7/16.
Wadsworth, Alfred, b. Leeds, e. Leeds, 32981, Pte., k. in a., F. & F., 3/5/17.
Waite,Wilfred, b. Guiseley, Yorks, e. Bradford (Bradford), 16/1036, Pte., k. in a., F. & F., 1/7/18.
Walker, Ernest, e. Chesterfield, 41717, Pte., k. in a., F. & F., 27/2/17, formerly 34315, Sherwood Foresters.
Walker, Harry, b. Leeds, e. Leeds, 32894, Pte., d., F. & F., 9/8/17.
Walker, Joseph, b. Hebden Bridge, Yorks, e. Halifax, 41673, Pte., k. in a., F. & F., 3/5/17, formerly 39607, K.O.Y.L.I.
Walker, Percy, b. Manningham, Bradford, Yorks, e. Bradford, 16/169, L/Sgt., k. in a., F. & F., 1/7/16.
Walmsley, Arthur, b. Bradford, e. Bradford, Yorks, 16/380, L/Cpl., k. in a., F. & F., 1/7/16.
Watkinson, John, b. Leeds, e Leeds, 31806, k. in a., F. & F., 3/5/17,
Watson, Charles Arthur, b. Baildon, Yorks, e. Bradford, 16/73, C.S.M., k. in a., F. & F., 1/7/16.
Weaver, Charles, b. Witney, Oxfordshire, e. Bradford, Yorks (Heckmondwike), 16/1631, Pte., k. in a., F. & F., 1/7/16.
Whitaker, Gordon Stanley, b. Wakefield, Yorks, e. Leeds (Leeds), 37457, Pte., k. in a., F. &F., 30/4/17.
Wightman, Alfred Affleck, b. Leeds, e. Leeds, 35629, Pte., k. in a., F. & F., 13/5/17.
Wilks, Walter, b. Leeds, e. Leeds, 33061, Pte., d., F. & F., 11/5/17.
Will, John William, b. Leeds, e. Bradford, Yorks (Bradford), 16/87, Pte., k. in a., F. & F., 3/5/17.
Williams, William, b. Bradford, e. Bradford, Yorks, 28726, Pte., k. in a., F. & F., 2/12/16.
Willis, Edgar, b. Bradford, e. Bradford, Yorks, 16/614, Pte., k. in a., F. & F., 1/7/16.
Wilson, George, b. Bradford, e. Bradford, Yorks, 16/82, L/Cpl., k. in a., F. & F., 1/7/16.
Wilson, Norris, b. Wistow, Selby, Yorks, e. Selby, 31986, Pte., k. in a., F. & F., 9/11/16.
Wood, James Preston, b. Bradford, e. Bradford, Yorks, 19983, Pte., d. of w., F. & F., 10/11/16.
Wood, Thomas Stanley, b. Scarborough, Yorks, e. Bradford (Beeston Hill, Leeds), 16/355, Pte., k. in a., F. & F., 1/7/16.
Woodhead, Ernest, b. Bradford, e. Bradford, Yorks, 16/469, Pte., k. in a., F. & F., 26/6/16.
Woodhouse, Francis John, b. Pontefract, Yorks, e. Bradford, Yorks (Bradford), 16/106, L/Sgt., d. of w., F. & F., 22/7/16.
Woodhouse, Norman, b. Bradford, e. Bradford, Yorks, 16/1435, Pte., k. in a., F. & F., 1/7/16.
Woodhouse, Walter, b. Bradford, e. Bradford, Yorks, 16/69, Pte., k. in a., F. & F., 1/7/16.
Woodrow, William, b. Bradford, e. Bradford, Yorks, 16/1397, Pte., k. in a., F. & F., 1/7/16.
Woods, Gilbert, b. Leeds, e. Leeds, 31968, Pte., k. in a., F. & F., 10/11/16.
Woodward, Samuel, b. Leeds, e. Leeds, 32895, Pte., k. in a., F. & F., 3/5/17.
Wormald, Walter, b. Leeds, e. Leeds, 23317, L/Cpl., d. of w., F. & F., 13/5/17.
Worth, Rowland, b. Leeds, e. Leeds, 40863, Pte., k. in a., F. & F., 27/2/17.
Wright, Samuel Horsley, b. York, e. York, 37506, Pte., d. of w., F. & F., 5/5/17.
Wright, Walter, b. Nun Monkton, York, e. Ripon, Yorks, 41305, Pte., d., F. & F., 5/8/17.
Young, John William, b. Cawood, York, e. York, 38635, Pte., k. in a., F. & F., 27/2/17.

18th Battalion.

Abey, Henry, b. Sunderland, e. York, 34991, Pte., k. in a., F. & F., 12/5/17.

Abbott, William Edwin, b. Wistow, Yorks, e. Bradford, Yorks (Bowling, Bradford), 18/625, A/Sgt., k. in a., F. & F., 30/6/16.

Alderton, Harry, b. Bradford, e. Bradford, Yorks (Manningham), 18/454, Pte., k. in a., F. & F., 1/7/16.

Allatt, Thomas Henry, b. Bradford, e. Bradford, Yorks, 18/248, Pte., k. in a., F. & F., 16/9/16.

Allerton, John William, b. Selby, Yorks, e. York, 17921, Pte., k. in a., F. & F., 10/5/17.

Allott, James, b. Pudsey, Yorks, e. Pudsey, Yorks, 33101, Pte., d. of w., F. & F., 25/10/16.

Ambler, Frederick Brammer, b. Sheffield, e. Bradford, Yorks, 18/1409, Pte., d., F. & F., 22/4/16.

Anderson, John William, b Burley-in-Wharfedale, Yorks, e. Hull, 34286, Pte., k. in a., F. & F., 3/5/17.

Applin, Harry Warren, b. Laisterdyke, Yorks, e. Bradford, Yorks, 18/1410, Pte., d. of w., F. & F., 15/7/16.

Arundale, George Amos, b. Seamer, Yorks, e. Yorks, 33327, Pte., k. in a., F. & F., 3/5/17.

Atkinson, William, b. Bradford, e. Bradford, Yorks, 18/1458, Pte., d. of w., F. & F., 25/10/16.

Auker, Frank, b. Bradford, Yorks (Laisterdyke, Yorks), 18/1569, Pte., k. in a., F. & F., 30/6/16.

Austin, William, b. Heanor, Derbyshire, e. Barnsley, Yorks, 22677, Pte., d. of w., F. & F., 24/5/16. formerly 23 York & Lancs Regt.

Barber, Edward, b. Batley, Yorks, e. Bradford, Yorks, 18/744, Pte., k. in a., F. & F., 1/7/16.

Barber, George Arthur, b. Chatham, Kent, e. Bradford, Yorks (Frizinghall, Yorks), 18/876, L/Sgt., d. of w., F. & F., 1/7/16.

Barker, Willie, b. Scholes, Yorks, e. Bradford, Yorks, 18/1164, Pte., d. of w., F. & F., 27/7/16.

Barnes, Charlie, b. Queensbury, Yorks, e. Bradford, Yorks, 18/1391, Pte., k. in a., F. & F., 1/7/16.

Barraclough, Norman, b. Buttershaw, Yorks, e. Bradford, Yorks, 18/1097, Pte., d. of w., F. & F., 25/10/16.

Barraclough, William, b. Bradford, e. Bradford, Yorks, 18/123, Pte., k. in a., F. & F., 24/4/16.

Barran, Morris, b. Farsley, Yorks, e, Bradford, Yorks (Rodley, Leeds), 20/136, Pte., k. in a., F. & F., 1/7/16.

Bateman, Percy, b. Wibsey, Yorks, e. Bradford, Yorks, 18/104, Cpl., d. of w., Home, 8/7/16.

Beaumont, Albert, Knottingley, Yorks, e. Pontefract, Yorks, 40774, Pte., d. of w., F. & F., 11/5/17, formerly 28334, K.R.R.

Beck, Harry, b. Bradford, e. Bradford, Yorks, 18/81, Pte., k. in a., F. & F., 1/7/16.

Bell, William Frederick, b. Middlesbrough, e. Middlesbrough, Yorks, 16361, Pte., d., F. & F, 10/4/17.

Betts, Ross, b. Scarborough, e. Scarborough, Yorks, 10375, Pte., F. & F., 27/7/16.

Biggins, Laurence Lyons, b. Hull, e. Bradford, Yorks, 18/71, L/Cpl., k. in a., F. & F., 27/5/16.

Binns, John Richard, b. Leeds, e. Leeds, 33111, Pte., k. in a., F. & F., 3/5/17.

Binns, Thomas, b. Hunslet, Yorks, e. Bradford, Yorks (Shipley, Yorks), 18/874, Pte., k. in a., F. & F., 30/6/16.

Birkill, Charles, b. Bradford, e. Bradford, Yorks, 18/875, C.S.M., k. in a., F. & F., 20/7/18.

Blow, John Thomas, b. Spalding, Lincs (Cowbit, Lincs), 457, Pte., d. of w., F. & F., 26/5/17, formerly 24914, Lincs Regt.

Booth, Edmund, b. Bradford, e. Bradford, Yorks, 18/190, Pte., k. in a., F. & F., 1/7/16.

Booth, George Herbert, b. Pudsey, Yorks, e. Bradford, Yorks, 18/296, Pte., k. in a., F & F., 1/7/16.

Bowskill, Arthur William, b. Mansfield, Notts, e. Bradford, Yorks, 18/1119, Pte., d. of w., F. & F., 1/7/16.

Bramhill, Thomas, e. Louth, Lincs (Louth), 40459, Pte., k. in a., F. & F., 3/5/17, formerly 25293, Lincs. Regt.

Brayshaw, John, b. Bradford, e. Bradford, Yorks, 41283, Pte., k. in a., F. & F., 3/5/17.

Brewer, Albert, b. Bradford, e. Bradford, Yorks, 20/155, Pte., k. in a., F. & F., 1/7/16.

Briggs, George, b. Leeds, e. Leeds, 33102, Pte., d. of w., F. & F., 1/5/17.

Briggs, Arthur, b. Bradford, e. Bradford, Yorks, 18/456, Pte., k. in a., F. & F., 24/4/16.

Britton, Charles, b. North Brierley, Yorks, e. Bradford, Yorks, 18/603, Pte., k. in a., F. & F., 3/5/17.

Broadley, John Ernest, e. Leeds (Leeds), 41287, Pte., k. in a., F. & F., 3/5/17.

Brock, James Edgar, b. Bradford, e. Bradford, Yorks, 18/993, Pte., k. in a., F. & F., 1/7/16.

Brogden, Thomas Blakey, b. Bradford, e. Bradford, Yorks, 18/950, Pte., k. in a., F. & F., 1/7/16.

Brown, Alfred, b. Retford, Notts., e. Bradford, Yorks, 18/431, Pte., d. of w., F. & F., 3/7/16.

Brown, Ernest, b. Bradford, e. Bradford, Yorks, 18/243, Pte., k. in a., F. & F., 3/7/17.

Brown, Frank Raper, b. Leeds, e. Leeds. 34209, Pte., k. in a., F. & F., 29/6/17.

Brown, Harold, b. Tong, Bradford. e. Bradford, Yorks, 18/952, L/Cpl., k. in a., F. & F., 3/5/17.

Brown, John, b. Castleton, Yorks, e. Bradford, 18/1487, Pte., k. in a., F. & F., 1/7/16.

Brown, Thomas, b. Mitford, Northumberland, e. Newcastle-on-Tyne, 47987, Pte., k. in a., F. & F., 3/5/17, formerly 32865, Yorkshire Regt.

Brunt, Arnold Vincent, b. Poole, Otley, Yorks, e. Bradford, 18/1331, Pte., k. in a., F. & F., 3/5/17.

Bryan, Joseph Henry, b. Bradford, e. Bradford, Yorks, 18/523, Pte., k. in a., F. & F., 3/5/17.

Burgoyne, Cyril Percival, b. Hull, e. Bradford, Yorks, 18/78, Cpl., k. in a., F. & F., 23/6/17.

Burley, Charles William, b. Grimsby, e. Bradford, Yorks, 18/1320, Pte., k. in a., F. & F., 30/4/17.

Burton, Norman, b. Clayton West, Yorks, e. Bradford, Yorks, 18/378, Pte., k. in a., F. & F., 1/7/16.

Burton, Samuel, b. Birkenhead, Cheshire, e. Bradford, Yorks, 18/1242, L/Cpl., d. of w., F. & F., 17/6/17.

Buswell, Ernest Victor, e. Leicester (Leicester), 40453, L/Cpl., d., F. & F., 3/5/17. formerly 30987, Leicestershire Regt.

Bywater, Walter, b. Low Moor, Yorks, e. Bradford, Yorks, 18/1460, Pte., k. in a., F. & F., 3/5/17.

Caley, Ernest William, b. Butley, Suffolk, e. Keighley (Keighley), 40329, Pte., d. of w., F. & F., 25/10/16.

Calvert, Herbert, b. Leeds, e. Leeds, 34482, Pte., k. in a., F. & F., 3/5/17.

Carter, Guy Ripley, e. Bradford (Bradford, Yorks), 40327, Pte., k. in a., F. & F., 13/11/16.

Cawthorne, Herbert, b. Bradford, e. Bradford, Yorks, 18/449, Pte., k. in a., F. & F., 1/7/16.

Caygill, Percy, e. York (Garforth, Yorks), 40304, Pte., k. in a., F. & F., 3/5/17.

Chambers, Arthur, e. Leeds (Hunslet, Yorks), 40252, Pte., d. of w., F. & F., 25/10/16.

Cheshire, Norman, b. Bradford, e. Bradford, Yorks, 18/697, Pte., k. in a., F. & F., 1/7/16.

Clark, John Robert, b. Nottingham, e. Nottingham, 47969, Pte., k. in a., F. & F., 3/5/17.

Clarke, Edward, b. Rossington, Yorks, e. Mexborough, Yorks, 27553, Pte., k. in a., F. & F., 2/3/17, formerly 22182, York & Lancs.

Clarkson, George, b. Masham, Yorks, e. Masham, Yorks, 33090, Pte., d. of w., F. & F., 12/5/17.

Clayburn, Joe, b. Bradford, e. Bradford, Yorks, 18/1415, Pte., k. in a., F. & F., 12/5/17.

Clayton, Horace, b. Luton, Beds., e. Bradford, Yorks, 18/844, Pte., k. in a., F. & F., 1/7/16.

Clegg, Joseph, b. Normanton, Yorks, e. Bradford, Yorks (Bradford), 18/879, Cpl., d. of w., F. & F., 1/7/16.

Clough, George, b. Bradford, e. Bradford, 18/507, Pte., k. in a., F. & F., 1/7/16.

Cockshott, Frank, b. Bradford, e. Bradford, Yorks, 18/902, Pte., k. in a., F. & F., 30/7/16.

Collinson, John Edward, b. Bradford, e. Bradford, Yorks, 18/1491, Pte., k. in a., F. & F., 25/2/17.

Cooke, Williamson, b. Leeds, e. Leeds, 29497, Pte., k. in a., F. & F., 12/5/17.

Coulson, George, b. Rothwell, Yorks, e. Leeds, 26275, Pte., d., F. & F., 15/9/16.

Craven, James, b. Bradford, e. Bradford, Yorks, 18/152, Pte., k. in a., F. & F., 1/7/16.

Craven, Wilfred, b. Bradford, e. Bradford, Yorks, 18/878, Pte., k. in a., F. & F., 30/6/16.

Craven, William Allen, b. Bradford, e. Bradford, Yorks, 18/667, Pte., k. in a., F. & F., 1/7/16.

Crerar, John, b. Bradford, e. Bradford, Yorks 18/997, Pte., d. of w., F. & F., 29/9/16.

Croft, Stanley, b. Bradford, e. Bradford, Yorks, 18/35, L/Cpl., k. in a., F. & F., 27/7/16.

Crossley, Herbert, b. Bradford, e. Bradford, Yorks, 18/683, Pte., k. in a., F. & F., 13/11/16.

Crossley, John William, b. Bradford, e. Bradford, Yorks, 18/17, Pte., d. of w., F. & F., 19/5/16.

Crotch, Ernest, b. Bradford, e. Bradford, Yorks, 18/525, Pte., k. in a., F. & F., 1/7/16.

Crowe, Norman, e. York (Bulmer, Yorks), 40269, Pte., k. in a., F. & F., 13/11/16.

Crowther-Clarance, b. Bradford, e. Bradford, Yorks, 18/672, Pte, k. in a., F. & F., 1/7/16.

Cullum, Harold, b. York, e. Bradford, Yorks, 18/1055, Pte., k. in a., F. & F., 18/8/16.

Cure, Vincent, b. Bradford, e. Bradford, Yorks, 18/1211, Pte., d. of w., F. & F., 3/7/16.

Darling, Horace, b Bradford, e. Bradford, Yorks, 18/1264, Pte., k. in a., F. & F., 13/11/16.

Davies, Henry, b. Aberystwyth, e. Hammersmith, 48007, Pte., k. in a., F. & F., 3/5/17, formerly PM2/230451, R.A.S.C. (M.T.).

Daybell, Arthur, b. Bradford, e. Bradford, Yorks, 18/187, Pte. k. in a., F. & F., 1/7/16.

Denton, Thomas William, b. Bradford, e. Bradford, Yorks, 18/148, L/Sgt., k. in a., F. & F., 3/5/17.

Dixon, Fred, b. Bradford, e. Bradford, Yorks, 18/479, Pte., k. in a., F. & F., 1/7/16.

Dixon, Wilfred, b. Morton, Yorks, e. Bradford, Yorks, 18/375, Pte., d. of w., F. & F., 20/5/16.

Donovan, William, b. Hillsborough Bks., Sheffield, e. Sheffield, 7252, Pte., k. in a., F. & F., 3/5/17.

Driver, Herbert, b. Bingley, Yorks, e. Keighley, Yorks, 18/1480, L/Cpl., k. in a., F. & F., 27/9/16.

Duggan, John, b. Greenock, Lanarks, e. Bradford, Yorks (Bradford), 18/624, Pte., d. of w., F. & F., 30/9/16.

Dunn, John, b. Leeds, e. Leeds, 33364, Pte., k. in a., F. & F., 3/5/17.

Dutton, Henry Frederick, b. Leicester, e. Leicester, 40462, Pte., d. of w., F. & F., 26/11/16, formerly 31024, Leicestershire Regt.

Dyson, Herbert, b. Bradford, e. Bradford, Yorks, 18/261, Sgt., k. in a., F. & F., 1/7/16. M.M.

Eccles, Harry, b. Woodley, e. Bradford (Bradford, Yorks), 18/1463, Pte., k. in a., F. & F., 10/6/16.

Ellis, Leslie, e. Pudsey Yorks (Bramley, Yorks), 41291, Pte., k. in a., F. & F., 3/5/17.

Fawcett, John, b. Castle Bolton, Yorks, e. Halifax (Skipton, Yorks), 40330, Pte., d. of w., F. & F., 16/6/17.

Fawcett, Joseph Robert, b. Bradford, e. Bradford, Yorks, 18/176, Pte., k. in a., F. & F., 1/7/16.

Fearnside, William Edward, e. Bradford (Bradford, Yorks), 40271, Pte., k. in a., F. & F., 3/5/17.

Ferguson, John, b. Sunderland, e. Leeds, 12870, L/Cpl., k. in a., F. & F., 3/5/17.

Ferrand, Claude Ernest, b. Bradford e. Bradford, Yorks, 18/252, Pte., k. in a., F. & F., 22/5/16.

Firth, Arthur, b. Bradford, e. Bradford, Yorks, 18/1076, Pte., k. in a., F. & F., 30/6/16.

Firth, Herbert, b. Birstall, Yorks, e. Bradford, Yorks, 18/1244, Cpl., d. of w., F. & F., 7/5/17.

Firth, Joseph, b. Baildon, Yorks, e. Bradford, Yorks, 20/169, Pte., d. of w., F. & F., 1/7/16.

Firth, Lewis, b. Bradford, e. Bradford, Yorks, 18/1167, Pte., d. of w., F. & F., 1/7/16.

Fisher, Alfred, e. Leicester (Leicester), 40467, Pte., k. in a., F. & F., 3/5/17 formerly 31009, Leicestershire Regt.

Forryan, Thomas, e. Leicester (South Knighton), 40468, Pte., d. of w., Home, 7/7/17, formerly 30997, Leicestershire Regt.

Fry, James, b. Bradford, e. Bradford, Yorks, 18/68, Pte., k. in a., F. & F., 28/4/16.

Garbutt, John, b. Southport, e. Bradford, Yorks (Bradford, Yorks), 18/638, L/Cpl., k. in a., F. & F., 1/7/16.

Garside, Ratcliffe, b. Bradford, e. Bradford, Yorks, 18/882, Pte., k. in a., F. & F., 27/8/16.

Gaunt, Joseph William, b. Bradford, e. Bradford, Yorks, 18/526, Pte., k. in a., F. & F., 3/7/17.

Gaunt, Leonard, b. Bradford, e. Bradford, Yorks, 18/405, Pte., k. in a., F. & F., 1/7/16.

Geeves, George, b. Bradford, e. Bradford, Yorks, 47992, Pte., d. of w., F. & F., 13/5/17, formerly 28960, Yorkshire Regt.

Gentle, Thomas Henry, b. Birmingham, e. Birmingham, 47926, Pte., k. in a., F. & F., 3/5/17, formerly M2/267871, R.A.S.C. (M.T.).

George, Edward Sydney, b. Birmingham, e. Birmingham, 47927, Pte., k. in a., F. & F., 3/5/17, formerly 229811, R.A.S.C.

Giles, Henry Edward, b. Ashford, e. Ashford, Kent, 325156, Pte., k. in a., F. & F., 28/1/18.

Gill, John, b. Silsden, Yorks, e. Keighley, Yorks, 18/836, Pte., d. of w., F. & F., 1/7/16.

Gill, Sam, b. Bradford, e. Bradford, Yorks, 18/783, Pte, d. of w., F. & F., 3/7/16.

Gillett, Herbert Elijah, b. Bradford, e. Bradford, Yorks, 20/26 Pte., k. in a., F. & F., 30/6/16.

Gledhill, Herbert, b. Bradford, e. Bradford,Yorks, 18/614, Pte., k. in a., F. & F., 1/7/16.

Gledhill, John, b. Adwalton, Bradford, e. Bradford, Yorks, 19/133, Pte., k. in a., F. & F., 3/5/17.

Goddard, Tom, b. Leicester, e. Leicester, 27329, Pte., k. in a., F. & F., 12/5/17.

Godridge, William Henry, b. New Wombwell, Yorks, e. Bradford, Yorks, 18/520, Pte., k. in a., F. & F., 3/5/17.

Goldthorpe, Walter, b. Sowerby Bridge, e. Bradford, Yorks (Bradford), 18/784, Pte., d. of w., F. & F., 1/7/16.

Gough, George Albert, b. Wolverhampton, Staffs, e. Bradford, Yorks, 18/555, Pte., d. of w., F. & F., 15/11/16.

Grant, Albert, b. Leeds, e. Leeds, 33377 ,Pte., d., F. & F., 11/12/16.

Grant, Richard, b. Leeds, e. Leeds, 48806, Pte., k. in a., F. & F., 8/2/18.

Grayson, Randolph, e. Leeds, 40302, Pte., k. in a., F. & F., 24/10/16.

Greasley, Joseph James, e. Leicester (Birstall, Leicester), 40475, Pte., k. in a., F. & F., 3/5/17, formerly 31129 Leicestershire Regt.

145

Green, Harry Charles, e. Bradford, Yorks, 18/193, Sgt., d. of w., F. & F., 22/6/16.

Green, Walter, b. Huddersfield, e. Halifax, Yorks, 32178, Pte., k. in a., F. & F., 13/11/16.

Greenwood, Henry Bernal, b. Bradford, e. Bradford, Yorks, 18/9, Sgt., k. in a., F. & F., 30/6/16.

Greenwood, Percival, b. Bradford, e. Bradford, Yorks, 18/906, Sgt., d. of w., F. & F., 5/5/17, M.M.

Gresswell, William Wood, e. Bradford, Yorks, 16/1728, Pte., k. in a., F. & F., 26/10/16.

Hackford, Frank, b. Martin, Doncaster, Yorks, e. Bradford, Yorks, 18/413, Pte., d. of w., F. & F., 6,7/16.

Hague, Harold, b. Sheffield, e. Sheffield, 9071, Pte., k. in a., F. & F., 1/7/16.

Haigh, Ernest Willie, b. Halifax, e. Halifax, Yorks, 40241, Pte., k. in a., F. & F., 12/5/17.

Haigh, Morris, b. Batley, Yorks, e. Bradford, Yorks, 18/1105, Pte., k. in a., F. & F., 27/7/16.

Haines, Walter B., b. Leeds, e. Leeds, 26277, Pte., d. of w., F. & F., 7/5/17.

Hallam, George b. Leeds, e. Leeds, 300070, Pte., k. in a., F. & F., 15/6/17.

Halliday, Samuel, b. Windhill, Yorks, e. Bradford, Yorks, 18/80, L/Cpl., d., Home, 10/11/15.

Hamblin, Hubert Charles, b. St. Albans, Herts, e. Bradford, Yorks, 18/196 C.S.M., k. in a., F. & F., 1/7/16.

Hamilton, William, b. Carrington, New South Wales, Australia, e. Newcastle-on-Tyne (Sunderland), 20269, Pte., k. in a., F. & F., 3/5/17.

Hammond, Percy, b. Farnley, Leeds, e. Bradford, Yorks, 18/206, Pte., k. in a., F. & F., 1/7/16.

Hanson, George James, b. Selby, e. Selby, Yorks (Cawood, Yorks), 33422, Pte., k. in a., F. & F., 3/5/17.

Hardwick, William Cyril, b. Leeds, e. Colsterdale, Yorks, 15/1269, L/Cpl., k. in a., F. & F., 3/5/17.

Hargreaves, Richard, b. Wyke, Yorks, e. Bradford, Yorks, 18/1107, Pte., d. of w., F. & F., 17/5/16.

Harper, John Abbotson, b. Giggleswick, Yorks, e. Keighley, Yorks, 20/145, Pte., k. in a., F. & F., 1/7/16.

Harriman, Elisha Horn, b. Hogsthorpe, Lincs, e. Spilsby, Lincs, 40482, Pte., d., F. & F., 5/2/17.

Harrison, Thomas Henry, b. Pudsey, Yorks, e. York, 41280, Pte., k. in a., F. & F., 3/5/17, M.M.

Hawkridge, James, b. Hopperton, Yorks, e. Harrogate, Yorks (Starbeck), 33402, Pte., d., F. & F., 5/5/17.

Hayes, Walter, b. Leeds., e. Leeds, 24254, L/Cpl., d. of w., F. & F., 27/10/16.

Haylock, Arthur, e. Bradford, Yorks, 40303, Pte., k. in a., F. & F., 13/11/16.

Haynes, John Edward, b. Kirkstall, Yorks, e. Bradford, Yorks, 18/940, Pte., k. in a., F. & F., 1/7/16.

Haynes, Robert William, b. Armley, Leeds, e. Leeds, 33112, Pte., k. in a., F. & F., 3/5/17.

Haywood, Bertie, b. Waxham, Norfolk, e. Leeds (West Hartlepool), 40258, L/Cpl., k. in a., F. & F., 26/10/16.

Hazlewood, Harry, b. Doncaster, e. Bradford, Yorks, 18/25, Pte., k. in a., F. & F., 3/9/16.

Heathcote, Dennis, b. Countesthorpe, Leicestershire, e. Leicester, 40479, Pte., k. in a., F. & F., 10/5/17, formerly, 31131, Leicestershire Regt.

Heeley, Robert, b. Bradford, e. Bradford, Yorks, 18/639, Pte., k. in a., F. & F., 3/5/17.

Hefford, Wilfred, b. Kettering, Northants, e. Leeds, 33183, Pte., k. in a., F. & F., 13/5/17.

Helliwell, Albert, b. Bradford, e. Bradford, Yorks, 18/1475, Pte., d. of w., F. & F., 6/7/16.

Helliwell, Maurice, b. Bradford, e. Bradford, Yorks, 18/279, Pte., k. in a., F. & F., 1/7/16.

Hill, Harry, b. Bradford, e. Bradford, Yorks, 18/1424, Cpl., k. in a., F. & F., 1/7/16.

Hill, John Henry, b. Bradford, e. Bradford, Yorks, 18/95, Pte., d. of w., F. & F., 27/4/16.

Hill, Norman, b. Bradford, e. Bradford, Yorks, 19/98, Pte., d. of w., F. & F., 6/7/16.

Hill, Thomas, b. Bradford, e. Bradford, Yorks, 18/1106, Pte., k. in a., F. & F., 1/7/16.

Hills, Harry, b. Bradford, e. Bradford, Yorks, 18/295, Pte., k. in a., F. & F., 1/7/16.

Hodgson, Joseph, b. Bradford, e. Bradford, Yorks, 18/1498, Pte., k. in a., F. & F., 1/7/16.

Hogan, William, b. Bradford, e. Bradford, Yorks, 18/1464, Pte., k. in a., F. & F., 17/6/17.

Holdsworth, Harry, b. Low Moor, Bradford, e. Bradford, Yorks, 18/126, Cpl., k. in a., F. & F., 1/7/16.

Hollingdrake, Walter, b. Bradford, e. Bradford, Yorks, 18/709, Pte., k. in a., F. & F., 3/5/17.

Holmes, John, b. Bradford, e. Bradford, Yorks, 18/1625, Pte., k. in a., F. & F., 1/7/16.

Hornsby, Joseph Edmund, b. Leeds, e. Leeds, 38687, Pte., d., F. & F., 21/2/17.

Horrocks, George, b. Bolton Woods, Yorks, e. Bradford, Yorks, 18/374, Pte., k. in a., F. & F., 1/7/16.

Houghton, John William, b. Metheringham, Lincs, e. Lincoln, 40481, Pte., k. in a., F. & F., 3/5/17, formerly 24931, 3/4 Lincs Regt.

Housecroft, Vincent, b. Drighlington, Yorks, e. Leeds, 26196, Pte., k. in a., F. & F., 3/5/17.

Hughes, Hughie, b. Beaumaris, Anglesey, e. Manchester, 20012, Cpl., k. in a., F. & F., 1/7/16, formerly 25081, 10th Hussars.

Hughes, Joseph Holmes, b. Whitby, Yorks, e. Leeds, 300040, Pte., k. in a., F. & F., 3/5/17.

Humphreys, Stanley, b. Bradford, e. Bradford, Yorks, 18/1132, Pte., k. in a., F. & F., 1/7/16.

Hurley, Herbert, b. Bradford, e. Bradford, Yorks, 18/1201, Pte., k. in a., F. & F., 3/5/17.

Hutchinson, Harrison, b. Bradford, e. Bradford, Yorks, 18/1594, Pte., d. of w., F. & F., 27/7/16.

Ingleson, Harvey Dixon, b. Leeds, e. Leeds, 300057, Pte., k. in a., F. & F., 15/6/17.

Jackson, Fred, b. Bradford, e. Bradford, Yorks, 18/1427, Pte., k. in a., F. & F., 1/7/16.

Jackson, James, b. Scarborough, e. Scarborough, Yorks, 12969, Pte., k. in a., F. & F., 3/5/17.

Jagger, George William, b. Bradford, e. Bradford, Yorks, 18/942, Pte., d. of w., F. & F., 1/7/16.

Jary, Robert Eldred, e. Boston, 40484, Pte., d., F. & F., 15/1/17.

Jeffery, Arthur, b. Blackheath, Kent, e. Lewisham, Kent, 40786, Pte., k. in a., F. & F., 3/5/17, formerly 26153, K.R.R.

Johnson, Arthur, b. Bradford, e. Bradford, Yorks, 18/975, L/Cpl., k. in a., F. & F., 1/7/16.

Johnson, Charlie, b. Bradford, e. Bradford, Yorks, 18/60, Sgt., k. in a., F. & F., 3/5/17.

Johnson, Herbert, b. Staveley, Westmorland, e. Keighley, Yorks (Keighley), 18/838, L/Cpl., k. in a., F. & F., 1/7/16.

Jones, William Harold, b. Llanrhaiardi, Denbighshire, e. Bradford, Yorks, 18/1269, Pte., k. in a., F. & F., 1/7/16.

Jordan, Arthur, b. Bradford, e. Bradford, Yorks, 18/1585, Pte., k. in a., F. & F., 1/7/16.

Jordon, William, b. Alnwick, Northumberland, e. Newcastle-ou-Tyne (Newcastle-on-Tyne), 47994, Pte., k. in a., F. & F., 3/5/17, formerly 32862, Yorks Regt.

Jowett, Frederick, b. Darlington, e, Bradford, Yorks (Bradford) 18/450, Pte., d. of w., F. &. F., 27/7/16.

Jowett, Thomas Lund, b. Pudsey, Yorks, e. Bradford, Yorks, 18/943, Pte., k. in a., F. & F., 1/7/16.

Joyce, Michael Henry, b. Bradford, e. Bradford, Yorks, 18/1523, L/Cpl., d. of w., F. & F., 3/7/16.

Kay, William Henry, e. Grantham (Grantham), 40486, Pte., k. in a., F. & F., 29/4/17, formerly 25204, 3/4th Lincs Regt.

Kellett, Walter Arnold, b. Wibsey, Yorks, e. Bradford, Yorks, 18/1343, Pte., k. in a., F. & F., 23/6/17.

Kendall, Harry, b. Queensbury, Yorks, e. Keighley (Keighley), 18/634, Drmr., k. in a., F. & F., 1/7/16.

Krause, Frederick Lewis, b. Nottingham, e. Nottingham, 27367, Pte., d. of w., F. & F., 1/3/17.

Langdale, Thomas, b. Welburn, Yorks, e. Beverley, Yorks, 23057, Pte., k. in a., F. & F., 25/2/17, formerly 19313, East Yorks Regt.

Lapish, Fred, b. Shipley, Yorks, e. Bradford, Yorks, 19/103, Pte., k. in a., F. & F., 13/11/16.

Larvin, James, e. York (York), 40266, Pte., d. of w., F. & F., 12/5/17.

Leckenby, Mark, b. Bramham, Yorks, e. York, 34478, Pte., d., F. & F., 3/5/17.

Lee, Arthur, b. Leicester, e. Leicester, 40489, Pte., k. in a., F. & F., 3/5/17, formerly 31175, Leicestershire Regt.

Lee, Joseph, b. Glenfield, Leicester, e. Leicester, 40488, Pte., k. in a., F. & F., 3/5/17, formerly 31165, Leicestershire Regt.

Lee, Wilfred, b. Liversedge, Yorks, e. Cleckheaton, Yorks, 18/1155, Pte., k. in a., F. & F., 12/5/17.

Lister, William Edward, b. Bradford, e. Bradford, Yorks, 18/1300, Pte., k. in a., F. & F., 1/7/16.

Littlewood, Tom Crowther, b. Skelmanthorpe, Yorks, e. Huddersfield, Yorks, 28457, Pte., d. of w., F. & F., 30/4/17.

Lockwood, Arthur Harling, e. Bradford, Yorks (Laisterdyke, Yorks), 18/61, Pte., k. in a., F. & F., 17/12/17.

Lowndes, Sam, b. Holmfirth, Yorks, e. Keighley, Yorks, 18/713, L/Cpl., k. in a., F. & F., 1/7/16.

McCaffrey, James, b. Leeds, e. Leeds, 19/229, Pte., d. of w., F. & F., 25/10/16.

McDonald, Joseph, b. Bradford, e. Bradford, Yorks, 18/1346, Pte., k. in a., F. & F., 1/7/16.

Macaulay, Kenneth, b. Keighley, e. Keighley, Yorks, 18/835, Pte., k. in a., F. & F., 30/6/16.

Margerison, John, b. Bradford, e. Bradford, Yorks, 18/49, Drmr., k. in a., F. & F., 1/7/16.

Marsden, Charles, b. Bradford, e. Bradford, Yorks, 18/1271, Pte., k. in a., F & F., 1/7/16.

Marshall, Leonard, b. Wibsey, Yorks, e. Bradford, Yorks, 18/335, Pte., k. in a., F. & F., 3/5/17.

THE BRADFORD PALS

Massen, Thomas, e. Bradford, Yorks (Bradford), 18/1010, Cpl., k. in a., F. & F., 1/7/16.

Mayne, John George, b. Walworth, London, e. Bradford, Yorks, 18/700, Sgt., d. of w., F. & F., 5/7/16.

Meays, Harry, b. Ackworth, Yorks, e. Bradford, 18/650, Pte., k. in a., F. & F., 30/6/16.

Melia, Patrick Franice, b. Wednesbury, Staffs, e. Middlesbrough, Yorks (Middlesbrough), 21330, Pte., d. of w., F. & F., 22/8/16.

Metcalfe, David, b. Bradford, e. Bradford, Yorks, 18/698, L/Cpl., k. in a., F. & F., 3/5/17.

Metcalfe, John, e. York (Wetherby, Yorks), 201568, Pte., k. in a., F. & F., 31/8/17.

Metcalfe, Willie, b. Bradford, e. Bradford, Yorks, 18/446, Pte., k. in a., F. & F., 1/7/16.

Midgley, Mark, b. Bilton, Yorks, e. Poppleton, Yorks (Rufforth Grange, York), 33394, Pte., d. of w., F. & F., 2/3/17.

Miller, Andrew, b. Leeds, e. Leeds, 34377, Pte., k. in a., F. & F., 3/5/17.

Millington, Charles, b. Retford, Notts, e. Retford, Notts, 47977, Pte., k. in a., F. & F., 3/5/17.

Milner, Frederick, b. Leeds, e. Pudsey, Yorks, 33198, Pte., d. of w., F. &F., 9/5/17.

Milner, Herbert, b. Fogley, Bradford, e. Bradford, Yorks, 18/237, Pte., k. in a., F. & F., 1/7/16.

Milnes, Richard, b. Bradford, e. Bradford, Yorks, 18/474, Sgt., d., Home, 29/6/15.

Millward, George, b. Sheffield, e. Sheffield, 47997, Pte., k. in a., F. & F., 3/5/17.

Minns, James, b. Whitechapel, Middlesex, e. London, 4/7904, Cpl., k. in a., F. & F., 3/5/17.

Mitchell, William Henry, b. Bradford, e. Bradford, Yorks, 29264, Pte., d. of w., F .& F., 25/10/16.

Moffett, Henry, b. South Shields, e. Sunderland, 3/8607, Pte., d. of w., F. & F., 5/5/17.

Morris, Edwin, b. Bradford, e. Bradford, Yorks, 18/271, Pte., d. of w., F. & F., 25/5/16.

Moroney, Thomas, b., Dublin, e. Halifax, Yorks, 22751, Pte., k. in a., F. & F., 3/5/17, formerly 3/15433, West Riding Regt.

Mountford, William Charles, b. Rotherhithe, Kent, e. Southwark, 40792, Pte., k. in a., F. & F., 15/6/17, formerly 27082, K.R.R.

Murgatroyd, Arthur Edgar, b. Bradford, e. Bradford, Yorks, 18/13, Pte., k. in a., F. & F., 1/7/16.

Muscroft, Lorry, b. Bradford, e. Bradford, Yorks, 18/1112, Pte., k. in a., F. & F., 1/7/16.

Neal, Richard, b. Birmingham, e. Birmingham, 47935, Pte., k. in a., F. & F., 3/5/17.

Newsome, Joseph, b. Dewsbury, Yorks, e. Pudsey, Yorks, 27182, Pte., k. in a., F. & F., 3/5/17.

Newton, John, b. Keighley, e. Keighley, Yorks, 18/1160, Pte., k. in a., F. & F., 14/7/16.

Nicholl, Herbert Howarth, b. Bramley, Yorks, e. Halifax, Yorks, 22908, L/Cpl., k. in a., F. & F., 3/5/17, formerly 10789, 1st G.B. West Riding Regt.

Nixon, William Roland, b. Rugby, e. Nottingham, 47978, Pte., k. in a., F. & F., 3/5/17.

Norman, William, b. St. Andrews, Leicester, e. Leicester, 40492, Pte., k. in a., F. & F., 3/5/17, formerly 30986, Leicestershire Regt.

Normington, Arthur, b. Bradford, e. Bradford, Yorks, 18/1374, Pte., d. of w., F. & F., 1/7/16.

Normington, Joseph, b. Bradford, e. Bradford, Yorks, 18/373, Sgt., k. in a., F. & F., 1/7/16.

North, John Richard, b. Liversedge, Yorks, e. Bradford, Yorks, 18/31, Pte., k. in a., F. & F., 1/7/16.

North, Reginald, b. Liversedge, Yorks, e. Bradford, Yorks, 18/40, Pte., k. in a., F. & F., 1/7/16.

Norton, Frederick, b. Leeds, e. Leeds, 300013, Pte., k. in a., F. & F., 3/5/17.

Nowland, Walter, b. Leeds, e. Leeds, 40247, Pte., k. in a., F. & F. 29/7/17.

Nuttall, Leonard, b. Bradford, e. Bradford, Yorks, 18/202, Pte., d. of w., F. & F., 27/4/16.

Oates, John Joseph, b. Evenwood, Durham, e. Normanton, Yorks, 40797, Pte., d. of w., F. & F., 24/11/16, formerly 28982, K.R.R.

O'Brien, James Hadcock, e. London (Huddersfield, Yorks), 40315, Pte., k. in a., F. & F., 13/11/16.

Ogley, Edwin Arthur, b. Heck, Yorks, e. Pontefract, Yorks, 40799, Pte., k. in a., F. & F., 29/7/17, formerly 28983, K.R.R.

Oyston, William Wadsworth, b. Armley, Leeds, e. Bradford, Yorks, 18/135, Cpl., k. in a., F. & F., 1/3/17.

Page, James William, b. Belvedere, Kent, e. Woolwich, 21443, Pte., d. of w., F. & F., 16/7/17.

Palframan, Gordon, b. Bradford, Yorks, e. Halifax, Yorks, 40246, Pte., k. in a., F. & F., 13/11/16.

Pape, Charles, b. Bradford, e. Bradford, Yorks, 18/860, Pte., k. in a., F. & F., 1/7/16.

Parkin, Charles, e. Leeds (Leeds), 40245, Pte., d. of w., F. & F., 16/11/16.

Parkin, Samuel Austin, b. Leeds, e. Leeds, 40256, Pte., k. in a., F. & F., 3/5/17.

Pass, Harry b. Burslem, Staffordshire, e. Bradford, Yorks, 18/626, C.S.M., d. of w., 5/7/16.

Patchett, Herbert, b. Bradford, e. Bradford, Yorks, 18/198, Pte., d. of w., F. & F., 21/5/17.

Paterson, George Alfred, b. Forest Gate, Essex, e. East Ham, 40821, Pte., k. in a., F. & F., 1/3/17, formerly 26056, K.R.R.

Payne, Frederick George, b. Leeds, e. Leeds, 34334, Pte., k. in a., F. & F., 3/5/17.

Pearson, Samuel Benjamin, b. Hull, e. Hull, 23059, Pte., k. in a., F. & F., 3/5/17, formerly 19498, East Yorks Regt.

Pennett, William, b. Bradford, e. Bradford, Yorks, 18/358, Pte., k. in a., F. & F., 1/7/16.

Pennington, William, b. Stanningley, Yorks, e. Pudsey, Yorks, 25308, d. of w., F. & F., 1/3/17.

Phillips, Thomas, b. Windhill, Yorks, e. Bradford, Yorks, 18/1013, Pte., k. in a., F. & F., 3/5/17.

Philpotts, George, e. Leeds, 300059, Pte., k. in a., F. & F., 3/5/17.

Pinder, Harold, b. Leeds, e. Leeds, 300032, Pte., k. in a., F. & F., 3/5/17.

Pipe, Harry, b. Bradford, e. Bradford, Yorks, 27487, Pte., d., F. & F., 4/5/17, formerly 19035, West Riding Regt.

Plows, Richard, b. Tadcaster, Yorks, e. Bradford, Yorks, 18/1381, L/Cpl., d. of w., F. & F., 27/5/16.

Poole, Gilbert Edward, b. Bristol, e. Bristol, 47937, Pte., k. in a., F. & F., 3/5/17.

Poole, Harry, b. Shipley, Yorks, e. Bradford, Yorks, 18/1303, Pte., k. in a., F. & F., 15/6/17.

Powell, Albert Edward, b. Stockton, Durham, e. Sunderland, 23061 Pte., d. of w., F. & F., 9/7/16, formerly 9/14511, East Yorks Regt.

Presland, Albert Maltman, b. Bradford, e. Bradford, Yorks, 18/912, Pte., d. of w., Home, 30/11/16.

Preston, John, b. Bradford, e. Bradford, Yorks, 18/802, Sgt., k. in a., F. & F., 3/5/17.

Preston, Robert, e. Harrogate, 40307, Pte., k. in a., F. & F., 13/11/16.

Pullan, Edgar, b. Pateley Bridge, e. Keighley, Yorks, 18/619, Pte., k. in a., F. & F., 13/11/16.

Ragg, Alfred Harry, e. Leicester (Leicester), 40498, Pte., k. in a., F. & F., 3/5/17, formerly 30996, Leicestershire Regt.

Redman, Harry, b. Wilsden, Yorks, e. Bradford, Yorks, 18/890, Pte. k. in a., F. & F., 1/7/16.

Reynolds, Arthur, b. Bradford, e. Bradford, Yorks, 18/1084, Pte., k. in a., F. & F., 1/7/16.

Richards, John Edward, b. Leeds, e. Leeds, 300065, Rfln., k. in a., F. & F., 29/4/17.

Richardson, Ernest, b. Leeds, e. Leeds, 300060, Pte., k. in a., F. & F., 3/5/17.

Riddiough, Ernest, b. Bradford, e. Bradford, Yorks, 18/966, Pte., k. in a., F. & F., 12/5/17.

Riley, Herbert Leonard, b. Bradford, e. Bradford, Yorks, 18/1015, Pte., k. in a., F. & F., 3/5/17.

Riley, Ralph, b. Bradford, e. Bradford, Yorks, 18/1085, Pte., d. of w., F. & F., 19/5/16.

Robinson, Frank, b. Halifax, e. Bradford, Yorks, 18/493, Pte., k. in a., F. & F., 16/9/16.

Robinson, Thomas Henry, b. Bradford, e. Bradford, Yorks, 18/195, Pte., k. in a., F. & F., 1/7/16.

Robson, Ernest, b. Bradford, e. Bradford, Yorks, 18/151, Pte., k. in a., F. & F., 1/7/16.

Rudd, Sydney, b. Leeds, e. Leeds, 36836, Pte., k. in a., F. & F., 2/3/17.

Rudstein, Solomon, b. Leeds, e. Belfast, 47940, Pte., k. in a., F. & F., 3/5/17, formerly M/2/229973, R.A.S.C.

Rumbold, William Edgar, b. Tadcaster, e. Tadcaster, Yorks, 23940, Pte., k. in a., F. & F., 27/7/16.

Rushworth, Charles, b. Bradford, e. Bradford, Yorks, 18/1205, Pte., k. in a., F. & F., 1/7/16.

Sansome, Frank, b. Bradford, e. Bradford, Yorks, 18/945, Pte., d. of w., F. & F., 4/7/16.

Saville, James William, b. Bradford, e. Bradford, Yorks, 18/776, Pte., k. in a., F. & F., 30/6/16.

Schofield, Leonard, b. Pudsey, Yorks, e. Bradford, Yorks, 18/1019, Pte., k. in a., F. & F., 15/6/17.

Schofield, Percy, b. Bradford, e. Bradford, Yorks, 18/2, L/Cpl., k. in a., F. & F., 19/5/16.

Senior, Fred., b. Leeds, e. Leeds, 25565, Pte., k. in a., F. & F., 3/5/17.

Shaw, Alfred, b. Nottingham, e. Nottingham, 47981, Pte., k. in a., F. & F., 3/5/17, formerly 68489, Sherwood Foresters.

Shaw, Charles, b. Bradford, e. Bradford, Yorks, 18/1641, Pte., d. of w., F. & F., 20/6/17.

Shaw, Fred., b. Batley, Yorks, e. Halifax, Yorks, 32534, Pte., k. in a., F. & F., 3/5/17.

Shaw, Herbert, e. Leeds (Leeds), 40238, Pte., k. in a., F. & F., 3/5/17.

Short, Ernest, e. Wainfleet, Lincolnshire, 40300, Pte., d. of w., F. & F., 12/5/17.

Shuttleworth, Thomas Whitaker, b. Kildwick, Yorks, e. Keighley, Yorks (Keighley), 18/1045, Pte., k. in a., F. & F., 1/5/16.

Sidebottom, Benjamin, b. Wakefield, e. Leeds, 300061, Pte., F. & F., 1/9/17.

Simpson, George, b. Leicester, e. Leicester, 40502, Pte., k. in a., F. & F., 3/5/17, formerly 31017, Leicestershire Regt.

Skirrow, Joe Forrest, b. Yeadon, Yorks, e. Bradford, Yorks, 18/1185, Pte., k. in a., F. & F., 1/7/16.

Slater, James William, b. Bradford, e. Bradford, Yorks, 18/982, Pte., k. in a., F. & F., 3/5/17.

Smart, Bertie, b. Leeds, e. Leeds, 36966, Pte., k. in a., F. & F., 10/5/17.

Smith, Fred., b. Leeds, e. Leeds (Armley, Leeds), 25035, Pte., k. in a., F. & F., 25/10/16.

Smith, Harold Howard, b. Bradford, e. Bradford, Yorks, 18/544, Pte., k. in a., F. & F., 1/7/16.

Smith, John Edward, b. Salford, Lancs. e. Keighley (Skipton, Yorks), 18/870, Pte., d. of w., Home, 7/10/16.

Spencer, Arthur, b. Leeds, e. Leeds, 300034, Pte., k. in a., F. & F., 3/5/17.

Spurr, John, b. Leeds, e. Leeds, 33114, Pte., k. in a., F. & F., 3/5/17.

Steedman, Frank, b. Leeds, e. Bradford, Yorks, 18/1291, Pte., k. in a., F. & F., 15/6/17.

Stenhouse, James Thomas, b. North Shields, e. Bradford, Yorks, 18/1325, L/Cpl., k. in a., F. & F., 27/9/16.

Stott, Tom, b. Harrogate, e. Knaresborough, 23928, Pte., d. of w., Home, 22/5/17.

Sunderland, Joseph, b. Armley, Leeds, e. Bradford, Yorks, 18/385, Pte., d., F. & F., 11/10/16.

Sutcliffe, Frank, b. Bradford, e. Bradford, Yorks, 18/1196, Pte., k. in a., F. & F., 3/9/16.

Sutcliffe, Harry, b. Leeds, e. Leeds, 40255, L/Cpl., d. of w., F. & F., 3/5/17, M.M.

Swaine, George Albert, b. Bradford, e. Bradford, Yorks, 18/1333, Pte., k. in a., F. & F., 1/7/16.

Swallow, James, b. Leeds, e. Leeds, 300035, Pte., k. in a., F. & F., 3/5/17.

Sykes, Craven, b. Leeds, e. Leeds, 35295, Pte., k. in a., F. & F., 25/2/17.

Symons, Frederick William Henry, b. St. Pancras, London, e. Marylebone, 22940, Pte., k. in a., F. & F., 3/5/17, formerly 15999, West Riding Regt.

Tarran, Arthur, b. Bradford, e. Bradford, Yorks, 18/790, Pte., k. in a., F. & F., 1/7/16.

Tate, Joseph, b. Bradford, e. Bradford, Yorks, 18/89, Pte., d. of w., F. & F., 30/6/16.

Tempest, David, b. Leeds, e. Leeds, 12135, Pte., d. of w., F. & F., 2/3/17.

Tempest, John Lawson, b. Otley, Yorks, e. Harrogate (Pannal, Yorks), 24392, L/Cpl., k. in a., F. & F., 31/5/17.

Thomas, Frederick Edward, b. Bradford, e. Bradford, Yorks, 18/530, Pte., k. in a., F. & F., 3/5/17.

(1556)

Thompson, Charles Frederick, b. Hull, e. Leeds (Hunslet, Yorks, 34383, Pte., k. in. a., F. & F., 3/5/17.

Thompson, Ernest, b. Huddersfield, e. Bradford, Yorks (Bradford), 18/893, Pte., k. in a., F. & F., 1/7/16.

Thompson, Horace, b. Bradford, e. Bradford, Yorks, 18/342, Pte., k. in a., F. & F., 1/7/16.

Thompson, James Henry, b. Bradford, e. Bradford, Yorks, 18/1434, Pte., k. in a., F. & F., 3/5/17.

Thornton, Charles Edward, b. Grimsby, Lincs. e. Richmond, Yorks, 26063, Pte., k. in a., F. & F., 19/10/17.

Tidswell, Herbert Bedford, b. Sowerby Bridge, Yorks, e. Halifax, Yorks, 40233, Pte., d. of w., F. & F., 13/11/16.

Tiplady, Ronald, b. Halifax, e. Halifax, Yorks, 40237, Pte., k. in a., F. & F., 3/5/17.

Topham, George Henry, b. York, e. Bradford, Yorks, 18/984, Pte., k. in a., F. & F., 1/7/16.

Tweedale, Sam, b. Manchester, e. Bradford, Yorks, 18/99, Pte., k. in a., F. & F., 23/6/17.

Tyerman, William, e. West Hartlepool (West Hartlepool), 40314, Pte., d. of w., F. & F., 4/3/17.

Upton, George Henry, b. Bermondsey, London, e. Bradford, Yorks, 18/140, Sgt., k. in a., F. & F., 27/7/16.

Varley, Herbert, b. Skipton, Yorks, e. Bradford, Yorks, 18/102, Pte., d. of w., F. & F., 17/6/17.

Vickerman, William, b. Hunmanby, Yorks, e. Scarborough, 21159, L/Cpl., d. of w., F. & F., 25/10/16.

Waddington, John, b. Bradford, e. Bradford, Yorks, 18/896, Pte., k. in a., F. & F., 1/7/16, D.C.M.

Walden, Ernest, b. Bradford, e. Bradford, Yorks, 18/357, A/Cpl., k. in a., F. & F., 22/5/16.

Walker, Harry, b. Bradford, Yorks, e. York, 19559, Pte., k. in a., F. & F., 1/7/16.

Walker, Stanley, b. Cleckheaton, e. Cleckheaton, Yorks, 20/191, Pte., k. in a., F. & F., 1/7/16.

Ward, John, e. Leeds, 300037, Pte., k. in a., F. & F., 3/5/17.

Watson, Donald, b. Hexham, Northumberland, e. Sunderland, 3/8787, Pte., k. in a., F. & F., 3/5/17.

Westwood, Joseph, b. Wombwell, Barnsley, Yorks, e. Houghton, 22707, Pte., k. in a., F. & F., 3/5/17.

Whitaker, Charles Gordon, b. Bradford, e. Bradford, Yorks, 18/245, L/Cpl., k. in a., F. & F., 27/7/16.

Whittaker, Harold, b. Sharleston, Yorks, e. Bradford, Yorks, 18/541, Pte., k. in a., F. & F., 1/7/16.

Whitaker, James, b. Denholme, Yorks, e. Keighley, Yorks, 18/1277, Pte., k. in a., F. & F., 1/7/16.

Whitaker, Willie, b. Wyke, Yorks, e. Bradford, Yorks, 18/596, Pte., k. in a., F. & F., 1/7/16.

White, Eric, b. Mendlesham, Suffolk, e. Bradford, Yorks, 18/1039,
   Pte., d. of w., F. & F., 8/7/16.
White, James Edward, b. Walworth, London, e. Kennington, 40816,
   Pte., k. in a., F. & F., 3/5/17, formerly 27031, K.R.R.
Widdop, Edwin, b. Bradford, e. Bradford, Yorks, 18/1186, Pte., k. in a.,
   F. & F., 1/7/16.
Wilkinson, Edgar, b. Bradford, e. Bradford, Yorks, 18/1127, Pte.,
   k. in a., F. & F., 27/7/16.
Wilkinson, William Child, b. Bradford, e. Bradford, Yorks, 18/867,
   Pte., k. in a., F. & F., 3/5/17.
Wilks, Francis William, b. York, e. Bradford, Yorks, 18/467, Pte.,
   k. in a., F. & F., 1/7/16.
Willan, John, b. Bradford, e. Bradford, Yorks, 18/1197, Pte., k. in a.,
   F. & F., 15/8/16.
Wilson, Arthur Snowden, b. Bradford, e. Bradford, Yorks, 18/1436,
   Cpl., d. of w., F. & F., 4/7/17, M.M.
Wilson, Fred, b. Leeds, e. Leeds, 300018, Pte., k. in a., F. & F., 3/5/17.
Wilson, Joseph, b. Leeds, e. Leeds, 36790, Pte, k. in a., F. & F., 3/5/17.
Winn, Joseph Luke, b. Nottingham, e. Nottingham, 47984, Pte., d. of w.,
   F. & F., 5/7/17.
Wise, Thomas, b. Ripon, e. Bradford, Yorks, 18/1128, L/Sgt., k. in a.,
   F. & F., 13/11/16.
Wood, Edward, b. Leeds, e. Leeds, 40342, Pte., k. in a., F. & F.,
   13/11/16.
Wood, John William, b. Middlesbrough, Yorks, e. Bradford, Yorks,
   18/274, Pte., d. of w., F. & F., 28/4/16.
Wood, Peter Barrett, b. Bradford, e. Bradford, Yorks, 18/564, Pte.,
   d. of w., F. & F., 18/8/16.
Wright, Harold, b. Addingham, Yorks, e. Bradford, Yorks, 18/189,
   L/Cpl., d. of w., Home, 15/7/16.
Yaffin, Jack, e. Leeds, 40301, Pte., k. in a., F. & F., 2/3/17.

READING LIST

GENERAL:

Malcolm Brown: Tommy goes to War: Dent & Sons, 1978. *Based on letters, diaries and reminiscences of the ordinary soldier.*

A.G.S. Enser: A subject bibliography of the First World War. 2nd edition. Gower, 1990. *A recent guide to the thousands of books written on the First World War.*

Norman Gladden: The Somme 1916: a personal account. W.Kimber, 1971? *One man's view*

Randel Gray: Chronicle of the First World War; 2 vols. Facts on File, 1990. A tabulated presentation of events.

Philip J.Haythornthwaite: The World War One source Book. Arms & Armour Press, 1992. *An excellent guide to events and sources.*

The Official History of the War. HMSO. *This multi-volume work was published over many years. The four volumes, 'Military Operations, France and Belgium, 1916,' covers the Battle of the Somme in detail.*

Terry Norman: The Hill they called High Wood. W.Kimber, 1984. *An account of a key area of the Battle of the Somme.*

A.J.P.Taylor: The First World War: an illustrated history. H.Hamilton, 1963. Penguin, 1960. *Popular account by a leading scholar.*

The Times History of the War; 22 volumes. The Times Newspaper. *An illustrated newspaper-type chronicle of events published soon after they happened. Gives a contemporary 'feel' to the war as it progressed.*

BRADFORD PALS AND THE WEST YORKSHIRE REGIMENT:

Bradford Citizens' Army League:.Report of the work of the league in assisting recruiting for the Navy and Army for service in the European War from Sept.1914 to March 1916 [1916]

Fred Conquest: Brief diary of Private Fred Conquest, 18th West Yorks. Regiment. Typescript, 1915.

Fred Raunsley: Diary of Fred Raunsley, Signal Section, 16th West Yorks. B.E.F. Typescript, 1916.

E.V.Tempest and E.C.Gregory: History of the Sixth Battalion West Yorkshire Regiment; 2 vols. Percy Lund Humphries, 1921-3. *Appendices list those who went abroad April 1915 (1/6th) and January 1917 (2/6th), officers, casualties and honours.*

War Diaries of the 16th and 18th West Yorkshire Regiment:

      Dec.1915 - Feb. 1916   WO 95/4590

      March 1916 - Feb.1918   WO 95/2362

(At the Public Record Office, Ruskin Avenue, Kew, Richmond, London, TW9 4DU. Copies can be seen at the Prince of Wales's Own Regiment of Yorkshire Museum, 3a, Tower Street, York, YO1 1SB)

Bradford Heritage Recording Unit recorded the memories of a few Bradford men who fought in the first World War. Transcripts of the interviews can be consulted in Bradford Reference Library

Everard Wyrall: The West Yorkshire Regiment in the War 1914-1918; Vol 1: 1914-1916; Vol 2: 1917-1918. John Lane, The Bodley Head, [1928]. *Appendices list casualties.*

BRADFORD DURING WORLD WAR I:

Allerton Congregational Church: Diary issued by the Men's Own Class Feb.1916-Jan.1919. *Contains news from home and abroad.*

Bradford Khaki Club: Wonderful story of voluntary labour in the Great War, 1915-1919. 1920. *This was a social club for soldiers and sailors.*

City of Bradford: Lady Mayoress's War Guild, including the wounded soldiers' personal comforts fund: Report. 1919

Charles Ogen: The Bradford war work souvenir. 1916. *Describes civilian work in Bradford with a list of voluntary war workers, and contains a chronological table of local war work events Aug.1914-June 1916.*

Richard I.Midgley: Attitudes towards the Great War in the City of Bradford 1914-1918. Typescript, 1987. *Huddersfield Polytechnic M.Phil thesis.*

Alan Smith: Bradford and the Great War: civilian response from Sarajevo to the Somme. Typescript, 1985? *B.A.thesis.*

COMMEMORATING AND LISTING SOLDIERS:

City of Bradford Roll of Honour Great War 1914-1918. *Lists, with brief details, most Bradford men who fought.*

The National Roll of the Great War 1914-1918. Section 9: Bradford. National Publishing Co., n.d. *Slightly fuller details of a small proportion of Bradford men who fought.*

Officers died in the Great War 1914-1919. HMSO, 1919. *List with very brief details and extracted in this volume.*

Soldiers died in the Great War 1914-1919. Part 19: The Prince of Wales's Own (West Yorkshire Regiment). HMSO, 1921. *List with very brief details. Sections for 16th and 18th Bns. reproduced here in full.*

Imperial War Graves Commission: The war graves of the British Empire: Great Britain and Ireland. Vol.8. 1931. *Includes soldiers buried in cemeteries and churchyards of Bradford. The Commission, now the Commonwealth War Graves Commission, 2, Marlow Road, Maidenhead, Berkshire, SL6 7DX, has published lists of all graves or memorial listings with brief information about each man.*

The unveiling of the Bradford War Memorial 1 July 1922. *Programme with a drawing of the memorial.*

Allerton and Daisy Hill War Memorial Souvenir 1914-1918, to commemorate the unveiling of the Allerton and Daisy Hill War Memorial 29 July 1922. *Details and photographs of those killed and names of those who fought.*

The Bradford newspapers published, often some weeks after the event, lists with brief details of men killed, wounded, missing etc.: Bradford Daily Argus, Bradford Daily Telegraph, Yorkshire Observer, Bradford Weekly Telegraph, Yorkshire Observer Budget. *The only index is to a series called "Our Gallant Heroes" in the Bradford Weekly Telegraph 1917 and 1918.*

OTHER POSSIBLE SOURCES OF INFORMATION:

Imperial War Museum, Lambeth Road, London, SE1 6HZ.

Liddle Collection of 1914-1918 Personal Experience Archives, University of Leeds Library, Leeds, LS2 9JT

Army Record Centre, Bourne Avenue, Hayes, Middlesex, UB3 1RF. *Holds those solders' papers from the First World War which have survived (perhaps 40%). They are confidential and information can be given only to next of kin. it is necessary to know the soldier's number and a charge is made.*

Public Record Office, Ruskin Avenue, Kew, Richmond, London, TW9 4DU *for the Medal Roll of the First World War which lists almost every soldier with brief details.*

General Register Office, St.Catherine's House, Kingsway, London, WC2 6JP *has separate indexes for the deaths of soldiers during the war.*

Norman Holding has written the following booklets published by the Federation of Family History Societies:

World War I army ancestry. 2nd ed. 1991

The location of British army records 1914-1918: *a national directory of World War I series.* 3rd ed. 1991

More records of World War I army ancestry. 2nd ed. 1991

INDEX OF MEN AND PLACES MENTIONED IN THE TEXT

Citations use either the form of name given in the text or a fuller form mentioned elsewhere if it is certain that reference is to the same person. There are inconsistencies and ambiguities even in the official sources so entries have been kept distinct where there is any question that reference is to different persons.